ADVENTURE IN NEEDLEPOINT

Wilhelmina Fox Feiner

ADVENTURE IN NEEDLEPOINT

Doubleday & Company, Inc.
Garden City, New York
1973

All photographs by Amandio de Sousa
ISBN 0-385-05983-3
Library of Congress Catalog Card Number 73-186019
Copyright © 1973 by Wilhelmina Fox Feiner
ALL RIGHTS RESERVED
PRINTED IN THE UNITED STATES OF AMERICA
FIRST EDITION

FOR *Sherry*
My Best Pupil

Contents

	Foreword	*ix*
	Preface	*xi*
I	*All about Canvas and Wool*	*1*
	Canvas	*1*
	Types and uses	*1*
	How to buy canvas	*4*
	Plan before you cut	*5*
	How to prepare your canvas	*8*
	Wool	*9*
	Types and uses	*10*
	Non-wool substitutes	*11*
	How to buy wool	*12*
	Sorting and storing wool	*13*
	A little more about wool	*14*
	What to do with leftovers	*16*
	Tools	*17*
II	*Your own Designs*	*19*
	How to find designs	*21*
	Materials required for designing	*22*
	Your mark	*23*
	Lettering	*23*
	Design Method 1	*25*
	To design a rug	*30*
	Design Method 2	*33*
	Design Method 3	*35*
	Painting your canvas	*36*
	Design Method 4	*36*
III	*All about Stitches*	*41*
	Threading your needle	*41*
	The basket-weave stitch	*43*
	A word to the left-handed	*46*
	Some handy thoughts about basket weave	*46*
	The continental stitch	*48*

	The brick stitch	50
	The Florentine family	53
	The Gobelin stitch	53
	Flame variations	55
	The herringbone stitch	57
	A few fancy stitches	58
	The Smyrna stitch	58
	The Scotch stitch	59
	The triangle stitch	60
	Borders	61
	How to make a braid trim	62
	How to make a cord	63
	How to make a tassel	66
IV	**Color**	69
	How to choose colors	69
	A few things you may not know about wool colors	70
	The company your colors keep	71
V	**Living with Needlepoint**	73
	Ideas and inspirations	74
	Projects	75
VI	**The Stand-ins**	81
	How by-products are born	83
	Traveling needlepoint	84
VII	**The Thought Counts**	85
	Make your gift a welcome one	85
	Gift ideas	86
VIII	**How to Cope with Disaster**	89
	How to avoid mistakes	90
	How to correct mistakes	91
	Some advice	93
IX	**Blocking**	95
	Instructions	96
	Equipment for blocking	98
X	**Mounting**	101
	Instructions	101
	How to restore your needlepoint	113
	Bibliography	114
	Index	115

Foreword

It wasn't altogether chance that made Wilhelmina choose Cat with Fish as her first example for transferring a design to canvas in *Adventure in Needlepoint*. I'm convinced that her interest in needlepointing dates from the evening some years ago when her beloved cat Irving took a fancy to a rug I was working on. I had put it on the floor to see how the work was progressing when Irving pounced on it, smelled the blue carnations, rolled all over it ecstatically and behaved as though he had just gotten stoned on catnip. It was at that particular moment (or so I would like to believe) that the author of this book, who is also my sister-in-law, decided she had better take up needlepointing or run the risk of losing Irving. As for the Fish part of the design—that was clearly thrown in because it's one of Irving's favorite foods and actually we should all be grateful to him for the part he played in being the catalyst for this delightful book.

Wilhelmina has been in love with the arts all her life and she has practiced them on both an amateur and a professional level. As an interior designer she combined taste and imagination with sound training and a practical sense of function. Her oldest and dearest hobby is gardening. She has the greenest of thumbs and I suspect she works a kind of magic by talking the flowers into blooming. But then she also does exquisite flower arrangements, dress designing and making, and she can prepare any number of delicious and unusual dinners. In all of these areas she is an amateur only in the true sense that she does these things for love—not money.

Since Wilhelmina is a woman of such extraordinary and varied skills, it came as no surprise to me that she had written this marvelously useful, lucid and charming book. There have been many excellent books about needlepoint published in the last few years and I have learned something from each one I've read, but *Adventure in Needlepoint* not only deals with all the aspects of working on canvas but it does so from a completely fresh and often unorthodox point of view. It has everything for the beginner and lots of good ideas, too, for those of us who have been doing needlepoint for years.

DOROTHY RODGERS

Preface

In her charming and flattering Foreword, my sister-in-law suggests I may have been led down the needlepoint path with my hand clutched tight in a furry paw. It is true that Irving took some sort of crazy trip among those blue carnations, but the rest of the story is purely fantasy.

That actual fact is, Dorothy herself showed me the beginning of the road sometime before Irving came into my life.

In the early years of our marriage, Ben and I lived in Southern California, and I wasn't very closely tuned to his sister's needlepoint projects. During a trip back to New York, I would observe that she was working on, for instance, a rug bordered with geraniums. Some months later, on a return visit, it would be finished and looking simply gorgeous on city or country floor. I greatly envied and admired the results of her talented stitches, and marveled over her ability to create these wonders. For some totally obscure reason, it never occurred to me that I, too, could make a rug with bright geraniums running around the edges. Acquiring the skill and cunning to produce such an *oeuvre* seemed as unattainable and improbable as learning to play the slide trombone, which is something I've very rarely thought of doing. (You must understand that all this was years before needlepoint madness swept the land, and Dorothy was the very first needlepointer I knew.) I was, besides, well enough occupied with a husband, a business, a house and a far-too-ambitious garden. My hands were not hanging limp for lack of something to keep them busy.

When Ben was assigned to the production of Winston Churchill's, *The Valiant Years,* we moved back to New York, and often spent weekends with the Rodgers at Rockmeadow. It was here I discovered that, basically, the art of needlepoint was only a matter of poking a needle through a fabric and pulling it out again. Since neither needles nor fabrics were strangers to me, I felt this mysterious process might prove not so difficult to learn as the slide trombone after all.

One weekend in particular stands clear in my memory. From Friday through to a Sunday evening, I watched Dorothy and another veteran needlepointer, Betty Furness, endlessly stitching with what might be described as serene intensity. Each, as I recall, was busy with a rug. Betty's was prodigious and exceedingly flowery, but I don't remember which of Dorothy's lovely small rugs was being born. I can, however, play back long, incomprehensibly esoteric discussions about the demerits of a background stitch she was using, and the final, earth-shattering decision to pick it all out and substitute another. She'd covered rather a large area and, in retrospect, I've been impressed by her courage.

It was during this weekend that Dorothy, who likes the look of idle hands even less than I, put a small, unfinished chair seat in mine and taught me the basket-weave stitch. I was now a member of the group and, as rows of snappy pink stitches grew, so did my resolve to needlepoint a project of my own. Visions of a rug the size of Betty's danced impractically in my head—to be finished within a few weeks, of course.

As I stitched, I delved into the economics of the craft. I asked a whole lot of general questions, and some very specific and personal ones too. After I'd digested the answers, my first adventure in needlepoint came to a stunningly abrupt end.

And that, really, is what this book is all about.

Several years passed before I found I could do needlepoint and still have enough money left over to buy a pair of shoes now and then. The precise moment of this discovery is dim as the wit which prevented me from making it earlier. Suddenly, it simply became perfectly clear that all the canvas I saw displayed in shop windows, pre-painted with rosebuds, spaniels, and replicas of the Mona Lisa must once have been virgin. Someone, somewhere put all those pictures on clean canvas which, surely, I reasoned, must cost a good deal less in a blank, untouched state.

My deduction, though tardy, was sound. The difference in price for canvas with and without the Mona Lisa was, indeed, astonishing—astronomically astonishing. So I figured out how to put my own ideas on canvas purchased by the yard. I relearned the basket-weave stitch, plus a few others, and, since that day, I've not been without at least one needlepoint project in the works, and a few more kicking around in my head.

Adventure in Needlepoint is the story of what I've learned by trial, error, experiment and experience. The book contains no history of needlepoint origins. There are no illustrations of fifteenth-century chasubles, ancient altar frontals or chairs embroidered by the daughters of the fifth marquess of Bath. It will only tell you the practical things I've discovered about planning, designing and stitching for *now*.

WILHELMINA FOX FEINER

Funchal, Madeira
1971

I

All about Canvas and Wool

Canvas

Because needlepoint canvas is woven and complete with warp, woof and selvage, it must qualify as cloth. However, I think of it only as a foundation—the skeletal framework on which the true fabric of needlepoint is constructed.

The meshes of this armature vary and, as with wool, you should cultivate a knowledge of each type and its possibilities.

Canvas is made from linen, cotton and, sometimes, Italian hemp threads, which are evenly spaced to form grids. These threads are heavily sized, or starched, so that the crossbars will stay firmly in place. Fresh off the roll, canvas looks and feels for all the world like window screening. After you've handled it a bit, it becomes a good deal more pliable.

Some canvas is white, which I contend is easiest on the eyes. Others vary from shades of ecru to a really nasty olive drab. All canvas is imported; usually from France or Germany, and it's relatively costly, so cherish it and waste not.

Types and uses

Canvas can be found in mesh counts from microscopic to mammoth. Counts specify the number of meshes, or squares, which occur in the space of 1 inch on your ruler. Thus, a 24-count canvas will have exactly 24 meshes to 1 inch, while a 3-count will measure 3 only.

A 10-count canvas—good for designs that are not too realistically complex.

A 12-count canvas—good for basket weave or any Florentine-bargello stitch.

The top count, or smallest mesh, is probably a gauze with something like 40 to the inch, but counts generally begin at a reasonable 24 for petit point, drop

ALL ABOUT CANVAS AND WOOL

to 16 (which is very petit point), then progress steadily downward to 14, 12, 10, 8, 6, 5, 4 and end with the quickest quick point, number 3.

Canvas widths vary too, and you can be fairly safe in following the rule that the smaller the mesh count, the narrower the canvas. Widths range from 24 to 40 inches, as a rule. Some petit-point canvas will measure less than 24 inches, and there's a rug canvas that jumps to 60. I've seen this last joined together and stretched on frames in rug factories, with workers ranged around them in quilting-bee style, but this width even unjoined doesn't exactly lend itself to comfortable lap work. I would avoid it.

A 14-count canvas—also excellent mesh count for basket weave and Florentine-bargello.

Regardless of width, mesh count or color, there are only two basic types of needlepoint canvas. One is made up of single, interwoven threads and is called *mono* canvas. The other doubles its threads and calls itself *Penelope*—in memory I suppose, of that legendary composite of irreproachable wife and patient weaver.

MONO CANVAS This good, serviceable, usually glistening white canvas can be purchased in nearly all the mesh counts aforementioned. By all odds, it's the most perfect surface on which to transfer your designs.

Both for basketweave and any of the Florentine-bargello stitches you'll be reading about, it's best of breed. The 14- and 12-count meshes are good for pillows and many another small article. The larger counts should be reserved for rugs, although 10-count is excellent for chair seats and even pillows if your design isn't too realistically complex.

A 16-count canvas—not as dense as true petit point (24 mesh) but the effect is very much the same.

PENELOPE CANVAS   It is said that the half-cross stitch can be worked successfully only on this double-thread canvas. Though I'm certain this information is correct, it does not induce me to rush out and buy Penelope canvas. Having experimented, I know the stitch pulls a canvas mercilessly out of shape, and a poor thing it is on its backside besides. The finished piece would wear very badly.

The second unique service this particular canvas can perform is infinitely more notable. The double set of threads allows you to work in stitches of two sizes in order to achieve greater detail along with textural variety.

What you will actually have is a design worked in petit point with a background area done in gros point. For the first, you will split the doubled threads; for the second, you will not. See Diagram page xx.

Whatever the mesh count, it works two ways in Penelope canvas. For example, a 10-20 mesh count will give you 20 stitches to 1 inch for your design, and 10 stitches to 1 inch for the background.

There's no reason, of course, why you can't do the entire project in 20-count petit point, but that's an awful lot of stitches to put into a canvas of any size.

How to buy canvas

Above all, when you select canvas, make certain it's free of knots, weak or uneven threads, flaws and sundry other imperfections. Examine it well *before* you allow it to be cut from the roll. Be rock firm about this. Smile, but insist.

As with wool, more often than not you'll find it fairly impossible to buy canvas to the last inch of your actual requirements, but you can (and certainly should) figure your area distribution before you make your purchase. This time a little simple arithmetic is necessary if you're to make the best use of your canvas yardage.

Plan before you cut

Some helpful suggestions for placement and cutting will be illustrated, but to describe a really elementary example, let us say you wish to make a pair of pillows which, when finished, will measure 14 inches square. The canvas you've chosen is 36 inches wide, so you'll buy a half yard and divide it into two equal parts. Allowing for a 2-inch border to be left unworked around those 14 inches, you will have used the half-yard investment to the conclusive last fraction. That will be that.

To progress to a second-grade equation, we'll assume you wish to make a pair of 18-inch square pillows. Again your canvas is 36 inches wide and, taking the unworked border into consideration, you will need a 22-inch square for each pillow. Since you can get only one of these squares from a width, you will buy 1-1/3 yards (you can't purchase canvas by inches). What you will actually need will be a length 44 inches by 22 inches, which will leave a 4-inch strip at the top. This you will stow away and, one day, you'll make a narrow belt. Had you splurged and bought 1½ yards, you'd have the makings of handsome wide belt.

In addition to this slender leftover, you'll have another, 14 inches wide and running the length of the two pillows. By no means look upon this as waste. Consider it a benison. This is "found" canvas, and many a small and charming project will evolve from this and subsequent dividends.

Don't hack wildly into a piece of canvas because you're in a hurry to begin a new venture. Study the area and think ahead to the possibility of making little economies.

Don't leave unnecessarily wide unworked portions around a designated outline. This *is* waste. Even if the surplus isn't very impressive, it may be quite enough for sandal straps or bands to trim a pair of pockets.

Don't hesitate to cheat a little. If a half inch less on each side of your margin will make the difference between a usable scrap and one fit only for the scrap basket, by all means help yourself.

Though I don't actually overbuy canvas, I like to have a few yards rolled, intact and on hand. Who knows when inspiration may creep up and clobber you? It's awfully satisfactory to begin any project while the fires of creation leap high.

* * *

The four diagrams will serve as theoretical examples of how best to utilize a minimum amount of canvas to maximum advantage. In each, the width of the canvas is 36 inches.

A is a plan for a needlepoint table top. The surface to be covered measures 40 by 21 inches so, allowing for 2 unworked inches at either end, plus an extra inch to provide for the thickness of the plywood (see instructions for table top page 111), 1¼ yards just does it. Since 26 inches are required for the width, this leaves you with a strip 10 inches wide by the length of the canvas: a perfect width for two belts. Allowing for a really ample waist measure, you still have a leftover leftover that is just right for front and back of an eyeglass case. Leave this scrap in one piece. You'll find it easier to work the two sections on the same canvas, and there's no reason to waste any of the area in hems you don't need.

B requires 1⅛ yards of canvas and a width of 22 inches to cut the two loose seat chair cushions in the diagrammed patterns. You now have a wider strip—14 inches to be exact—from which you can salvage two nice little pillows approximately 8 by 11 inches (note that I've indicated a narrower unworked margin around these. You don't need two inches for anything so small). Now you have a good-sized rectangle that is precisely the right dimension for making four

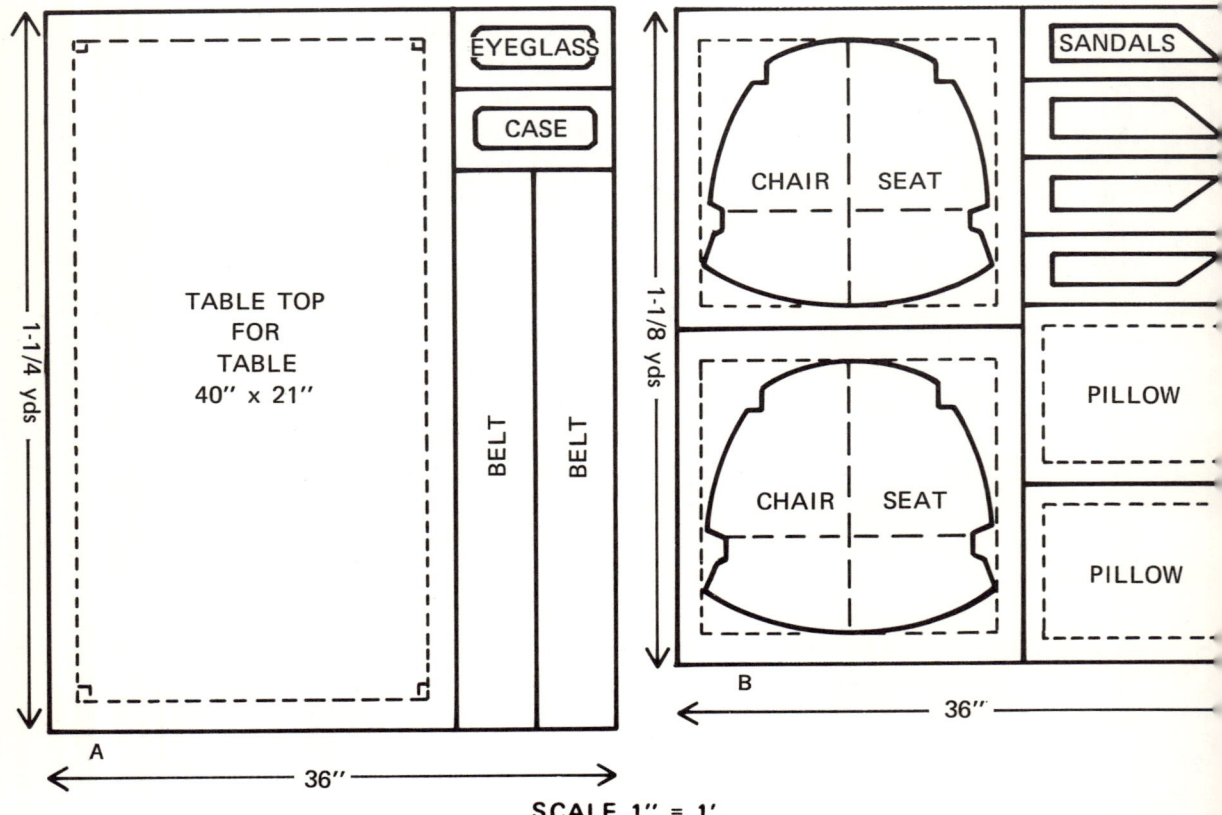

Scaled diagram for table top measuring 40 by 21 inches.

Suggestions for a chair seat cut from 36-inch-wide canvas. Notice how the leftover can be used for sandal straps and as a pillow.

ALL ABOUT CANVAS AND WOOL

sandal straps to the pattern on page 6. Don't cut these apart. Work them in one piece and you'll have zero waste. You'll save precious canvas by simply finishing off the outer edges. The 1½ inches you'd lose if you hemmed each section separately could, in many instances, make an enormous difference.

C presents a very simple non-problem involving two 16-inch square pillows. These fit exactly into a 1⅛-yard length of canvas, and will give you a beautiful, 16-inch dividend. Any number of interesting projects can evolve from an area of this size, but I chose to make a pair of smaller pillows and a little envelope purse.

D leaves you with very little in excess of what's needed to lay out the main project. The pattern is the one cut for the armchair on page xx and it required 1½ yards of canvas. The sole dividend here is a small strip from which I shall one day make bands to trim a pair of pockets. The black areas represent waste, though I do admit to having filed the 3- by 5-inch scrap. Who knows? As for the other sections, I simply moved the seat pattern to the center of the canvas

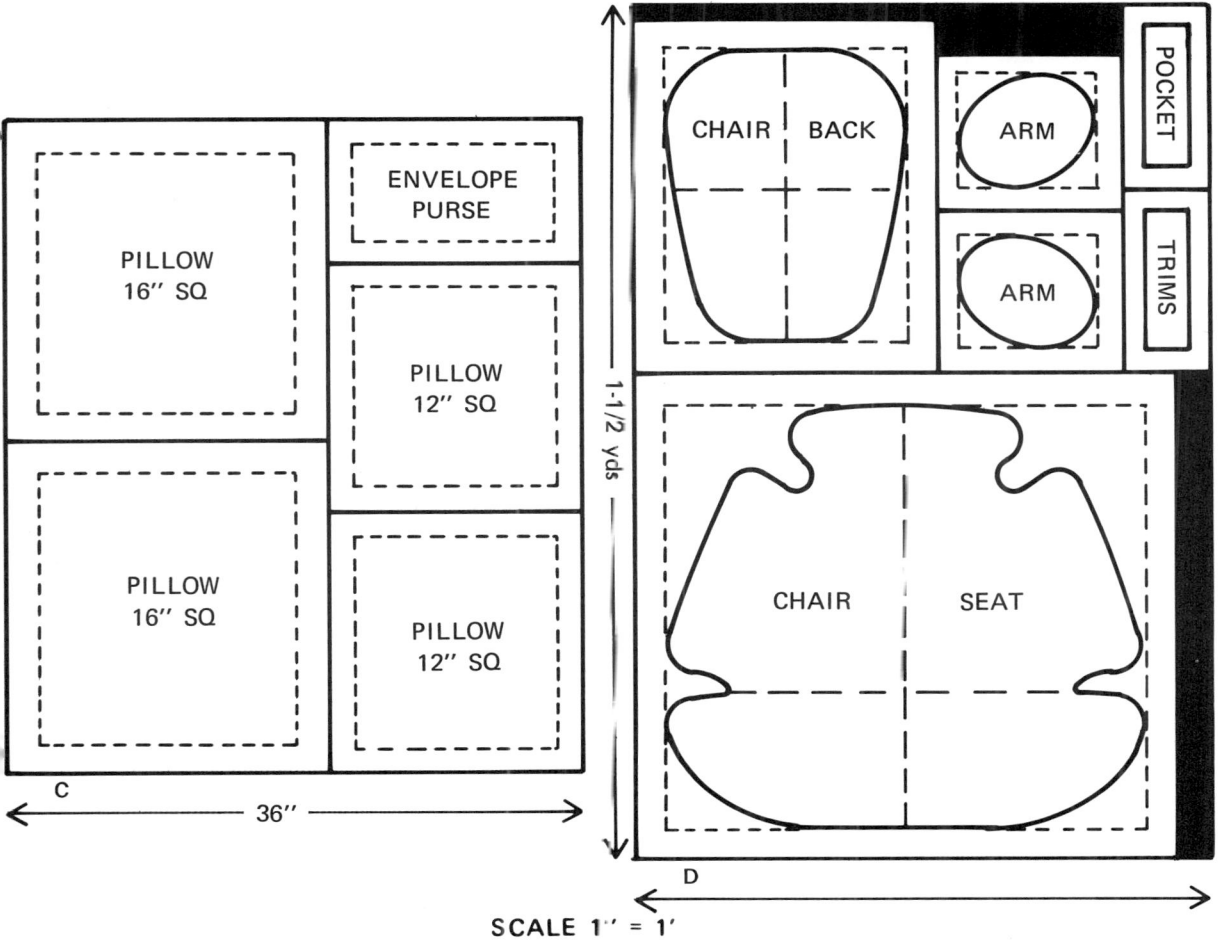

a 36-inch-wide canvas is purchased for a 16-inch square pillow, then there will be enough leftover canvas for perhaps a smaller pillow plus some.

Even if most of the canvas is used for your pattern, the small bit of leftover might be just enough for a decorative pocket trim.

so that I have selvages at either side, and gave myself an additional fraction for the back section.

This may be an unnecessary admonition but, when you're cutting to an eccentric shape (as in the three chair seats diagrammed), don't try to save canvas by lopping off corners. You'll need the full square or rectangle for blocking.

How to prepare your canvas

Although this reminder is probably gratuitous, don't forget you will always cut your canvas most carefully, using a marked row of meshes as the guideline from which you will never stray.

Once cut to size, it's immediately necessary to finish the raw edges in some fashion. You'll do this, please, even before you transfer your design. If you don't, the threads will begin to ravel with alarming rapidity as the canvas is handled.

There are specific solutions for preventing this fraying, and needlepointers differ about which is the most effective. Having tried each procedure at one time or another, I will give you my own findings. You can make your choice—or your own experiments.

The application of inch-wide masking tape is an accepted and popular finish, and it's used by a great many needlepointers. Simply double the tape over the canvas edges—half on one side, half on the other to serve as a binding. This is a quick method, accomplished in a matter of only a few minutes. The tape will stay securely affixed while you work, and until the finished piece is wet for blocking. At this point, your binding will float languidly away, leaving you with those same frayed ends it was meant to protect. This is messy, and it can be perilous.

There are those who recommend a thin line of liquid glue run around the cut canvas edges. To be sure, the glue will lock the threads and prevent raveling. However, it won't cover up those barbed ends. They'll grab your yarn and hold it like brambles. Besides, the glue dissolves when you wet your canvas, so any advantages this method may offer are far outweighed by it's deficiencies.

Hemming the canvas edges works best for me. The result is neat, it's safe, and its efficacy doesn't desert through working, to blocking, to final mounting. Turn the raw edges under about a quarter of an inch, and use the zigzag attachment on your sewing machine. If your machine isn't equipped with this handy accessory, make several rows of wide gauge stitches around the hem. Even if you don't own a sewing machine, all is not lost. A couple of rows of loose backstitches put in with a heavy linen thread will serve you well. They needn't even be very neat—just firm.

I stated earlier that you should allow 2 inches of unworked margin around your piece. Some needlepointers insist 3 inches is a minimum allowance, though I can't for the life of me think why. This seems a monumental waste and, for me,

ALL ABOUT CANVAS AND WOOL

2 is quite sufficient even for a large undertaking. If there's a selvage on one side, I'll leave a little less there since it's all firmly battened down anyway.

As for margins around those leftover bits and pieces, I've often given myself as little as 1 inch on all sides. The sky has not fallen, nor have my projects suffered any terrible fates. The little ones can't take very long to do, so they won't be handled much and, further, even most of that inch is going to be whacked off in mounting. Not playing by the rules has paid off in many a dividend.

Just incidentally, if I'm hemming a large piece of canvas, I also hem any small ones I have around at the same time so they'll stay intact for future use.

Wool

There are several different types of wool sold expressly for needlepoint. Accept no substitutes. Knitting yarn is made for knitting. The fibers are twisted together in short lengths, and the yarn would quickly disintegrate under the strain of being pulled, time after time, through sharp, starched canvas meshes. Yarns made exclusively for needlepoint are the ones you'll choose.

Although you will select your wool in direct ratio to the mesh count of the particular canvas on which you plan to work, you must learn that most yarns can accommodate themselves to smaller or larger counts. The parent strand may be separated, doubled or even tripled.

Familiarize yourself with the capacities and limitations of each variety, and make your selection accordingly.

Relation of wool and needle sizes to canvas mesh.

Types and uses

PERSIAN WOOL   This is the all-purpose, all-round choice for a great many needlepointers. It's durable, adaptable and obliging. In these respects, it is unique. The yarn is three-ply. That is to say, it's made up of three strands. These are rolled so loosely together, you'll find separating them is no trick at all.

Just as it comes from the hank, Persian wool is the perfect thickness and weight for a 10-count canvas.

For both 12 and 14, two of the three plies cover the canvas splendidly.

One single ply is used for petit point.

Two or three entire strands can combine successfully to cover 5- to 6-count rug canvas. The wool is tough, so you needn't be concerned about relentless feet marching across your creation when it's complete and on the floor.

Though you can buy Persian wool in an excellent range of colors, you may find it's not graded closely enough for you to achieve the absolute ultimate in realistic shading. Since it splits so readily, colors and tones can be combined for greater subtlety. See page xx.

This paragon of wools is made in New York City by the Paternayan Brothers, and blessings on them. Paternayan is strictly wholesale, so you won't be able to buy directly from the source. However, any needlework shop worth beans is well stocked with the product, and you'll have no trouble tracking it down almost anywhere in the United States.

TAPESTRY WOOL   Until I came to live in Madeira, I'd never worked with this excellent yarn. Now, I use it exclusively, and for a very good reason. Aside from rug wool, it's the only yarn available.

The yarn is made up of four rather tightly twisted plies, and it's considerably softer in texture than Persian wool. However, because it's used here for the manufacture of the finest of hand-made rugs, it is evidently durable.

Just as you buy it, the wool is perfection for covering a 12-count canvas. If you don't work too tightly, it will serve as well for 10-count.

While it's possible to separate the four plies, either for mixing or for use on finer canvas, it's an irritating job for anyone with only two hands. If you attempt to pull them apart, the strands twist willfully back into place, they snarl, and just generally behave abominably. With that third hand, the process is somewhat easier. Ask someone to hold one end while you split the threads, two and two. Sometimes you can do this in one quick and easy zip—sometimes not.

As an alternate suggestion, hold two plies in your right hand and, ever so gently, peel the other two down as though you were removing an opera-length glove. Follow the same procedure if you want three plies, but throw the fourth away. It will be too whispy and fragile for use.

I have read that tapestry wool—as is—is suitable for 14-count canvas. If you plan to work in the basketsweave stitch, I disagree. Not only will the stitches look lumpy, you'll find the canvas threads will begin to bunch together after you've worked only a few rows. While three of the four plies work up perfectly on 14-count, it would be folly to waste time peeling off hundreds upon hundreds of single threads. You could do this for your design alone, then work the background in brick stitch, which behaves quite nicely in its four-ply state. Better still, I think, use another type of yarn.

The tapestry wool I work with is mostly of Portuguese manufacture which, in quality and color range, is on a par with its American counterpart. In other words, very good indeed. However, the rug factory here, which so graciously allows me to purchase wools, has filled in with a number of shades from the French firm Bon Pasteur. I hold the thought that new ones will be added from time to time. The tones are so delicately graded that, to look at their color chart is to dream of actually painting in wool.

These same Bon Pasteur yarns can be obtained in the United States.

CREWEL WOOL   This yarn, as the name clearly suggests, is made primarily for crewel embroidery, but it's excellent for needlepoint too.

The wool is two-ply (not to be separated), and you would use a single strand for petit point. Two strands are generally sufficient to cover a 14-count canvas but, since I've found this yarn varies in thickness more than any other type, you may sometimes need three. The colors are particularly glorious and, if you come across an English import, you'll find the dyes intensely vibrant.

RUG WOOL   This is a four-ply yarn. It's heavier in texture and far tougher than ordinary needlepoint wool. Use it in a single strand for any rug mesh from 8 down through 5. Paternayan makes a fine rug wool too.

QUICK-POINT WOOL   This yarn is so thick you could hang the Monday wash on it, and the 3-count canvas you'd use with it might easily enclose a chicken run. As you may imagine, such a combination will give you minimum detail along with maximum speed—if that's what you're after.

Non-wool substitutes

EMBROIDERY FLOSS   Try DMC or Coats & Clark mercerized cotton floss for highlights and texture variations. It comes in six-ply strands and has a soft, silky sheen.

Separated, this is medium popular with petit pointers, but all six plies used together are just great for 14-count canvas, while four plies are right for 16 count. If your project is fairly small, you might use the floss for the entire area but, remember, it's packaged in skeins of only eight yards and this won't take you far. For a sizable undertaking, you'll need to buy in job lots.

FILOSELLE SILK   Again, this is a material used mostly for petit point, but it's awfully handy for picking out accents in more ample ventures. The silk is a French import and it's rather expensive. Doing an entire piece of needlepoint in this medium is something of an extravagance and, to handle, it's the most difficult thread on the list. It must be constantly smoothed, petted and pampered as you work.

How to buy wool

Since I am admittedly hopeless at solving problems involving barrels of apples, pounds of feathers, or speeding trains, I feel there's not much reason why I should be any good with the mathematics of figuring exactly how much wool I'll need for the pillow I'm about to make. You may as well ask me, "How high is up?"

I know, theoretically, that in order to come up with a true equation, I must first measure the amount of wool required to fill one square inch of my canvas. I will then proceed to determine the number of square inches I wish to cover. This result will now be multiplied by the length of the strand of wool used for that sample square inch and, with a bit more effort, I will convert those astronomical inches into yards.

The question now involves weights as well as measures. How many yards of the particular wool I plan to use make a pound? It's extremely unlikely that I know the answer, so I will call the wool shop and ask.

If you're still with me you'll see that only a little additional arithmetic is required, and I'll have the answer. Let's say I know for sure I'll need seven eighths of a pound of wool to cover my pillow. That is, of course, if I plan to do all the stitches in one single color.

I examine my sketch, and it's plain to see my background cuts in, out and around the central motif. It fills up in-between spaces and, just generally, distributes itself in a random sort of way. As for the design, it will be worked in three shades of bronze and two of olive. Surrounding this, I have indicated a cartouche in which I plan to use a number of shades of green, together with smallish spots of reds, ranging from salmon to deep coral.

Clearly, even with this imaginary creation, I've long since abandoned any attempt to decide how best to apportion that seven-eighths pound of wool.

I suggest a far simpler method, and one which will greatly insure your sanity. Take your full-scale sketch and color indication to your nearest needlework shop. Someone there will cheerfully judge the amount of wool you'll need for each area, usually with amazing accuracy. Cultivate a friendly, knowledgeable salesperson who will also be happy to dig out a missing color, or help you decide which shade will come closest to your original concept.

Soon enough your own eye will become accustomed to making the same sort of professionally correct approximation, and you'll be independently expert.

Whether you or another makes the calculation, always buy more than you think you need. Although color runs are a good deal more dependable than they used to be (until fairly recently, a new dye lot was invariably three shades off) you can always count on a slight variation. Though the difference seen in the skein may be imperceptible, the first rows stitched with the new lot can be most noticeably "off" from the old. Where an expanse of background is involved, in diagonal basket weave the changeover can become your bar sinister.

Now that I've been thoroughly logical about buying more than you've judged you'll need for a project, I may as well admit that I consistently and premeditatively overbuy. I suggest you do the same. If I am profligate, it's not only as insurance against running short, nor is it even because of my arithmetical blind spot. I simply like to build up and continually add to a private stock of wool.

If this method of buying sounds extravagant, let me assure you it is not. I can truthfully say I have found (or will find) a very good use for every surplus strand; and I literally mean every strand. Even when there are only three or four left over in the end, these are tied together and preserved. You never know when those few will be precisely right for a bright highlight, a deep shadow, a bit of this or that. For years I dipped into some surplus midnight blue I'd originally bought for the first pair of pillows I ever made. The last threads went into the spots on the dog and serpent in the Chinese wall hanging. That particular color served me well and often. I shall miss it.

Aside from these handy terminal scraps, I like having a small hoard of wools out of which many a new project can be built. Unless I need a large amount of yarn to cover a vast, ambitious background, or some very special color is missing from my stock, I shop at home where I can experiment at my creative leisure.

As you lock the last stitch in whatever you may be doing at the moment, don't despair if you find yourself with surplus wool. Rejoice, instead. Your next piece of needlepoint may well come in for free.

Sorting and storing wool

After you've completed several needlepoint projects, you'll have the nucleus for your stock pile of leftover wool. This will represent a growing investment, and you'll treat the accumulation with the utmost care and consideration. You must never allow it to become a woolly minestrone.

At the outset, sorting shades and colors won't present much of a problem but time will pass. Each completed venture will leave its trail of unused yarn. Not only will you want this excess readily available, you'll want it in the best possible condition. Sort each different leftover carefully and separately. Knot the strands loosely together, or tie them gently in the middle with a short piece of yarn.

Plastic bags were my first solution to the problem of how to isolate colors. All shades of blue went into one bag; greens into another, and so on. The idea seemed supremely practical until one day I realized my wool was beginning to mat. Evidently it needed to breathe. My wool was literally suffocating, so I abandoned the bags except for temporary use. They're invaluable for protecting and organizing work-in-progress. As a permanent residence, forget them.

If you're fortunate enough to have one or two deep drawers at your disposal, you're home free as far as storage is concerned. Lidded wicker baskets are good as well as decorative, if you have room for them. Should you be pushed to the limit for space, use an under-bed storage unit, or blanket boxes on accessible shelves.

Larger amounts of leftovers can simply be lumped into heaps, roughly according to color. To segregate the smaller bits, put a few lidless boxes inside your larger containers. Pale to deep shades of pink will go into one, for instance; beiges in another, thus making it an easy job to find just what you need without having to scramble through a variagated mess. In a word—organize!

These days, wools are treated against moths, but I take no chances. The proofing may not be forever and, when I think of the lavish dinner parties that might take place among my treasured yarns, I throw in a few moth crystals for added insurance and untroubled sleep.

A little more about wool

If your canvas threads show through as you work, one of two things is wrong. Either your wool isn't the proper thickness, or you're pulling your yarn too tightly. If the fault lies with the first, experiment with an added ply. If it's the second; relax.

When you're using very dark colors you'll cover the canvas better if you work with a little less than your usual tension. Consciously loosen up for these areas and you'll avoid those scattered white flecks.

* * *

If you have any difficulty in pulling your yarn through the canvas meshes, it's too heavy for the count. It should offer no resistance. Reduce the plies.

* * *

Given any choice at all in the matter, don't select wools from the short lengths bunched together on a sample card. It's virtually impossible to get the true feeling for texture or color.

* * *

Don't waste wool. Long years ago, when the art of needlepoint was young, yarn fatigued very easily. It became thin and frail as it traveled through the meshes, and it was necessary to retire the strand long before it lived a rich, full life. Happily, this is no longer the case. Your wool will remain quite plump and strong unto the last fraction of its length, so it's good economy and common sense to get the most you can from every possible inch.

A friend, who used to spend an occasional needlepointing evening with me, invariably left a heap of 5- to 7-inch lengths of multicolored discards behind. No amount of reasoning or scolding ever altered this shocking procedure, and I still shed a tear for the countless inches of canvas which could have been covered by those squanderings.

* * *

I've often read that it's against some law of needlepointing to mix wool types, but I look on this as one made to be broken.

If I am working primarily with tapestry yarn, but the very color I need for some area turns up in crewel wool, you can be certain I'll use it. Should I be doing a canvas in Persian wool, I'll ring in either or both other types if it suits my purpose and fancy. When the thickness of the yarns is matched by addition or subtraction of plies, I can perceive no visible difference in the quality of my stitches. Nor, I prefer to believe, can anyone else.

I don't mean I recommend actually setting out to mix wool qualities indiscriminately and in large expanses. If you need a considerable amount of a particular color, you won't fool around with odd lots in your own stock. You'll go out and buy what you want in the same type of wool you're using for the body of the piece you're making. However, should your problem concern itself with the shading of a flower, a bunch of leaves, the motif in a border or the wing of an angel, you may mix as you will with good effect and clear conscience.

* * *

Always be certain you're buying the best possible brand of yarn that can be had. If you know your source to be reputable, you should have no qualm, but beware of wool bought in any store or department which doesn't specialize in needlepoint supplies. I once trotted into a small notions shop which I knew sold tapestry yarn in small skeins. I needed ever so little of a color I didn't have, and I wanted it in a hurry. It was a deep crimson to shade some cherries, and the fruit came out round as real. My pleasure in it lasted just until I wet the finished piece for blocking. The background was a pale, pale blue, and—but need I go on?

Even an absolute guarantee of color fastness can't do a thing to restore your stitches, or repay you for the hours spent putting them in. Fortunately, you need very rarely worry about transient dyes these days, but bleeding does still occur from time to time. If you have any doubt at all, test the wool first. Leave nothing to chance.

* * *

Never reuse a strand of wool you've picked out of your canvas in order to correct an error. It will be weak as well as fuzzy.

* * *

Your wool will have a tendency to twist as you work. Remember to drop the strand from time to time. The weight of the needle will allow it to unwind, uncurl and fatten itself.

What to do with leftovers

Odd bits of this-and-that you find in your refrigerator can very often be transformed into something cleverly gourmet, and the same thing is true of wool and canvas scraps you've salvaged from some major project. Just as what evolves out of Saturday's leg of lamb will often be more exciting than the original roast, so the exquisite little pair of pillows you create spontaneously may give you more pleasure than the big, important job for which you purchased the canvas initially.

In the beginning of this chapter, you learned how to avoid canvas waste by plotting placement instead of cutting with careless abandon. You know all the good reasons for guarding and treasuring every last strand of wool, and you know how to sort and store it too. To preserve canvas remnants for the future, I find the most efficient method is to keep them flat in a small artists' portfolio. The long, narrow strips can be rolled and secured with a bit of yarn but, whatever the shape and size, and however you stow it away, the important thing is to finish off the raw edges of the canvas first. Left on its own, the piece will ravel and disintegrate. The useful will be rendered useless in no time flat so, when you hem or tape the boundaries of your main feature, do the same for any by-product. Should you be moved to transfer a design before you store any small canvas, you're that much ahead but, locking raw edges is immediately and absolutely essential.

Don't cast away anything that's large enough to put a few square inches of stitches into—it could turn into a crazy pincushion. A strip $3\frac{1}{2}$ inches by $6\frac{1}{2}$ inches—give or take a little—will make up into a band to trim the top of a pocket, while a 7- by 9-inch piece can become a whole patch pocket. Nine inches by ten (or even less) is quite big enough for a mini pillow, and long strips for belts can be almost any width, from $3\frac{1}{2}$ to 6 inches—length, of course, will be dictated by girth and the sort of buckle you've chosen. Just allow an unworked inch at either end—an inch all round is sufficient margin, as a matter of fact.

If you find you've only enough canvas for one pocket, or two sandal straps instead of four, be patient. The mates are quite apt to appear the next time you cut into a canvas with the same mesh count.

The beauty of this saving plan is, when you need that small bit of needlepoint to take on a trip, to have as a gift, or just for a stand-in, all the makings will be right at hand and in your own store.

A few of the ways you can turn found canvas scraps to profitable use are listed below, and you may think of several in addition. Some of these ideas are uni-sexed, **if you change the sizes and style a little.**

ALL ABOUT CANVAS AND WOOL

BELTS—all widths
STRAPS FOR LUGGAGE RACKS
SMALL PURSES
POCKET TRIMS—edges or flaps
PATCH POCKETS
MINI PILLOWS
STRAPS FOR SCUFF-TYPE SANDALS
SLIPPERS—only fine canvas for these (16 count)
EYEGLASS CASES—all sizes from Ben Franklins to shades
DOG COLLARS—why not? But not cat collars—cats should never wear them

Tools

Aside from wool, canvas and ten clever fingers, you'll need very little in the way of needlepoint equipment. Your work bag should contain the following:

SCISSORS: These must be small and sharp-pointed. The type sold for embroidery are best. You will use a larger, sturdier pair for cutting canvas.

NEEDLES: If you plan to work on a variety of canvas meshes—from petit point to quick point—you'll need a selection of needles numbering 22 to 13. For canvases with meshes 14-, 12- and 10-count, number 18 needles are interchangeable. Store your spares in small plastic pill bottles.

THIMBLE: Use a thimble if you need to, and many needlepointers do. Though I couldn't sew a single ordinary sewing stitch without this protection, I find myself hampered when I try to use one for needlepoint. Experiment to find out whether a thimbled or thimbleless middle finger suits you best.

TWEEZERS: These are very handy for picking out stitches after they've been clipped for removal.

EMERY BOARD: Always keep one of these in your work bag. It's to be used on *you*, not on your needlepoint. Wool fibers catching in a nicked nail are murder so, at the first sign of roughness, whip out the emery board. It will keep both your manicure and your temper smooth.

II

Your own Designs

When I was a little girl, my mother said to me, "Coloring books are trashy things. How will you ever learn anything by filling in a bad drawing somebody else has made?"

Mother was an extraordinarily early advocate of creative freedom for children, so color me fortunate. I never had a coloring book.

Now, many years later, and with much the same philosophy, I'm a snob about ready-to-work needlepoint canvases.

This is not to say all pre-painted, pre-prepared canvases are bad. On the contrary, many are well designed and freshly conceived—but not by you.

No matter how handsome or imaginative the piece you select from the shelves of your needlework shop may be, you know its multiple waits for a multiple stitcher. The pillow with the splash of daisies you lovingly worked into a yellow background might well turn up on the sofa of a friend. Perhaps she placed her daisies on hot pink, but this little variation won't alter the fact that the shape and direction of each leaf and petal will be acutely and cruelly familiar. To your sorrow, you'll realize that, having come to the end of painstaking hours as countless as your stitches, you've really only "filled in a drawing somebody else has made."

In addition to the nice feeling of having designed and made something unique, there's the not so small matter of a large cost differential between the *prêt-à-porter* canvas and the one you originate yourself. The variance may mean no more than a nifty little dividend. On the other hand, it could be as basic as finding yourself able to afford to do needlepoint and, alas, not being able to afford to do needlepoint at all.

Though saving is its own reward and never to be lightly looked upon, your most important satisfaction will lie in the knowledge that, from first stitch to final blocking, you've created something that's entirely and proudly *yours*.

It is true that there are needlepointers who take their own totally individual inspirations to be interpreted and transferred to canvas by a shop professional. There's no question about the fact that this method produces an original result, but there's an obvious drawback. The cost for such a service is fancy on an understandably grand scale; one which makes the ready-to-work piece seem a wild bargain by comparison. While I acknowledge and respect the fundamental originality of this high-income bracket form of needlepoint design, could I afford the indulgence, I believe I should still prefer my own very personal formula for trapping ideas.

* * *

This chapter isn't intended to be an art lesson. It won't teach you a thing about anatomy, nor will it instruct you in the principles of perspective. However, barring the possibility that each of your two hands is equipped with five chubby thumbs (in which case you wouldn't be very likely to attempt needlepoint in the first place), it will show you how to create, adapt or copy designs suitable for working in wool. It will teach you some tricks and techniques for transferring these designs to canvas. It will even hold your hand a little for guidance, comfort and encouragement.

If you have a built-in ability to draw and paint, you're way ahead. You'll simply learn to apply your skills in a new and interesting fashion. Using a needle as your brush, the transition from painting to embroidery is minimal. You'll find your "paint" has astonishing warmth and depth as well as a tactile quality unlike that of any medium I know. The range of color is immense, and those huge bins of brilliant to pale pastel skeins that line the walls of needlework shops are sheer inspirational heaven.

It isn't essential or especially important to have had instruction in any of the arts in order to design your own canvases and, if you don't feel the fires of latent talent smoldering inside you, never mind that. What *is* essential is that you give the formation and translation of your project a good deal of preliminary thought and care.

Remember, *always*, how much simpler it is to begin again on a fresh sheet of paper until you're certain of what you want, than it is to pick out innumerable stitches later on. This isn't very good for your canvas, and it's absolutely terrible for your disposition. Worst of all, you might find yourself faced with the ultimate tragedy; a completed piece you unreservedly and passionately loathe only because you didn't take the time to think out and properly plan the basic concept. It could turn you off needlepoint forever!

YOUR OWN DESIGNS

How to find designs

To begin, find an idea—or let an idea find you. It doesn't matter which comes first as long as you and a good formative notion get together and make friends.

Storing bright thoughts in a paper folder will keep them from drifting away. Whenever I look inside my head and find it empty as my canvas, I shuffle through clippings I've clipped and sketches I've sketched in search of a suggestion or the seed of an invention. The quest has never failed me.

One day, perhaps, the folder will grow up to be a proper file with tidy categories from Asphodels through Bugs and on to Zodiac, all neatly tabbed and alphabetically indexed, but I doubt this will ever happen. I suspect a preference for the grab-bag confusion of random oddments that have caught my fancy; clippings from magazines and newspapers, quick shorthand notes made in museums. Anything that once appealed to me in theory, may become a fact and, more often than not, it does.

The folder holds a casual and not very consistent assortment: an architectural fragment, a section of a cave painting, photographs of high-fashion models wearing interesting prints, the detail of an ancient carving, a mosaic, animals of all varieties, flowers, a dragon, a dragonfly. Most of these filed ideas are intended to be adapted or combined, but I very often steal them outright.

Many art books, publications and gallery catalogs are valuable sources for needlepoint suggestions. You can find handbooks of ornament (sometimes in cut-rate bookstores) and these are useful for helping you work out geometric borders and classic forms of all sorts. Old herbals are loaded with ideas, and even seed catalogs can contribute. Illustrated children's books are surprisingly serviceable, especially when they picture birds, beasts and nature's wonders in general.

The list is endless. An abstract painting can springboard you into something fabulous, but so can a parquet floor, a primitive tile, an Axminster carpet or the label on a can of beans.

I'm not forgetting adaptations of motifs from the living room chintz or the bedroom wallpaper, but this device has been mentioned elsewhere pretty often. I think most needlepointers have explored the possibilities of blowing-up or isolating a portion of a familiar design, but if you haven't thought of it, do.

The subject you choose to interpret may be traditional, frankly pretty or brilliantly and radically contemporary. Your colors may be gaudy or tender; primary or neutral. In the end, what appeals to you most strongly is what you'll most enjoy doing. It's as simple as that and, when you come right down to it, it's what modern needlepoint is all about anyway.

* * *

Before you decide on your initial project let me advise you to begin with a design that's more or less stylized. Clean, spare lines will be easy to transfer, and mass areas of color will be simple to "read" as you work. Save the subtleties of shading and intricacies of detail for later creations when you're more certain about your skills and are at ease with the essential materials. Keep this first choice bright and rather simple. Instead of finding yourself bewildered, bored or discouraged, you'll feel you're most awfully clever and talented. And so you are!

Materials required for designing

The materials you'll need for designing and transferring are inexpensive investments and can be purchased in any art supply store.

> A drawing board at least 18 by 24 inches.
> Rustproof aluminum drawing pins (*not* thumbtacks).
> A pad of newsprint paper for experimental sketches.
> A large pad of tracing paper—or a roll.
> Graph paper—for geometrics and lettering.
> Soft pencils—for sketching.
> A thin-line felt pen—black.
> A thin-line felt pen—gray.
> A roll of 1-inch masking tape.
> A ruler or yardstick—or both.
> A plastic triangle—or two of different sizes.
> A soft eraser, or kneaded rubber.
> Colored felt pens, or an inexpensive set of water color paints.

If you'd like to paint your canvas, I'll take up ways, means and additional materials later on in this chapter. Actually, I strongly advise that you do not apply paint. I find following a rigidly uncompromising placement of each shade and tone is limiting and sometimes even confusing.

However, should you feel you'd be happier working on a painted canvas, you'll still begin with the following basic steps and the supplies listed above.

The first two items—the drawing board and the aluminum pins—play a double role. They'll be used for blocking your finished canvas when the time comes.

The colored felt pens and/or water colors are meant for experimenting only—to indicate color decisions on a drawing or chart. They're definitely *never* to be applied to the canvas.

The black felt pen is best for making the final strong outline on tracing paper.

The gray felt pen will be used for the last, vital step of transferring your drawing to canvas. The pale indications will show up clearly but, at the same time, they won't assert themselves. Even though you can buy felt pens which are guaranteed waterproof (no matter what they say, better test them), I find a strong outline can be too insistent. Should you decide to extend an area a little, or to stop short of the boundary you've drawn, there's always the risk that the shadow of a dark line underneath will show through a light-colored wool. The pale gray tracing is safe; it'll give you freedom of choice and a free hand.

Whatever you do, don't be carried away and reach for the first handy pen when you're ready for your final transfer to canvas. Be certain it's waterproof so you can also be certain it won't bleed into your stitches when the piece has been wet for blocking.

I cannot stress this strongly enough and, if I sound like the voice of doom, it is with reason. I have the proof of several rather ugly incidents to back up my warnings.

Your mark

You created it. You stitched it into being. Now, the finished work deserves your signature.

Signing a piece of needlepoint and signing a painting are pretty much the same thing. The difference lies in the fact that, while this is usually the final brush stroke on a painter's canvas, a needlepoint signature should be planned ahead. In fact, it's a good idea to indicate its position and dimension on your preliminary tracing paper design.

There's nothing to be said against using two or three plain block letters ranged side-by-side or stacked one over the other, along with the date. However, if you find your initials lend themselves to some uncomplicated but distinctive coupling, so much the better. The signature will became a hallmark. Play around with combinations on graph paper, and you may come up with something interesting.

My own mark (Fig. 1, after p. 32) has undergone small changes and minor evolutions, but the basic arrangement of a W surmounting back-to-back Fs has remained essentially the same for years. The version I now use grew out of the Chinese wall hanging because I felt something with the look of an oriental chop might be appropriate. Since I find it neat and legible in any style, the chop has been my signet ever since.

Even if you stick to plain initials, it's better not to let them float around loose on your canvas. Put them in a tidy little box, and fill it in with a shade of wool just a little different from your background stitches.

Whatever you do, the signature shouldn't be too important or overpowering. It's only a means of signing your work, after all. You don't want it up in lights.

Lettering

There are times when you may want to use letters for something more than a signature. You're constantly expressing yourself in needlepoint, but you never know when you might actually want to *say* something in stitches. For this you will need to learn a needlepoint alphabet.

The formation of letters isn't always as easy as it seems. You can be as free as you like with paper and pencil, but those canvas meshes will dictate the direction your letters will follow. Some transfer themselves with orderly logic, while others, like A, V and W will sprawl all over if you don't compress them.

For the most part, it's best to stick to the simplest shapes. Add serifs to fancy

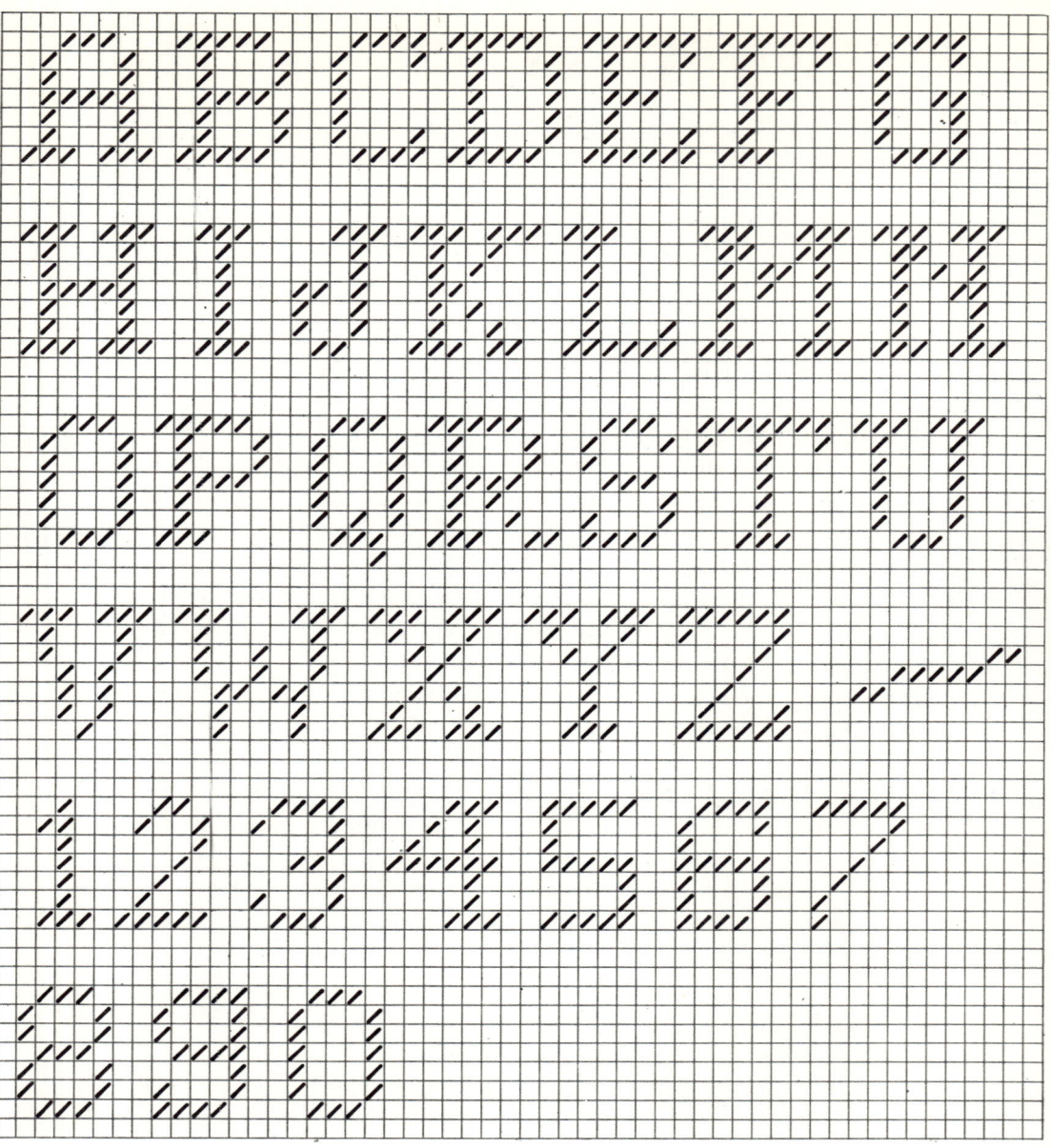

Basic pattern for the alphabet and numbers. Keep it simple to be effective.

up the letters, if you like, but stay clear of elaborately scrolled Spencerian script and Gothic swirls. The basic alphabet and unassuming numbers will start you off, but you may evolve some twists of your own on graph paper. Incidentally, anyone can draw letters this way. Counting the predetermined squares on paper and recounting them in canvas meshes requires zero talent.

Should you want to say something important enough to merit ornamental capitals, I've found alphabets in books like *Handbook of Ornaments* and *Monograms and Ciphers** which have inspired me. True, you can't reproduce all those fancy flourishes and interlacings in stitches but, if you reduce the curves and adapt them to graph paper limitations, you can come up with some pretty creditable calligraphy.

*Both books printed by Dover Publications, Inc., New York City.

Design Method 1

The evolution of Cat and Fish (Fig. 2, after p. 32) will serve as an effective guide. Follow it from the conception of the idea to ultimate stitch and you will have had your first lesson in how to transfer inspiration to canvas.

It all began with the small reproduction of a primitive Indian painting I found in *Time* magazine during the spring of 1968. When I saw it, it spoke to me in needlepoint language and was promptly clipped for the folder. The accompanying article told me the cat is held in reverence by the Bengalis of Calcutta because it's the mount of Shasti, the Bengalese goddess of fecundity. Mount of Shasti, or plain cat, I liked the design and thought it would work well on a pillow one day.

The painting wasn't graduated from the folder until the following November when I was searching for something with simple color masses and a lot of mindless background to take with me on a trip. I figured *Time* wouldn't mind and I was certain the folk artist, back in his aboriginal Indian settlement, might even be rather pleased if he knew his cat was about to have a reincarnation in stitches.

In order to keep the flimsy clipping intact, my first step was to mount it on a piece of cardboard. I wanted it uncrumpled and un-lost during its travels for I would need it as a constant reference wherever and whenever I wanted to needlepoint. Even if you aren't planning to leave home base, mounting is a good preservative measure.

Next, the clipping was enlarged photostatically to the size I wanted. The 5-inch figure grew to 13.

This enlarging process is invaluable to the designing needlepointer. Very often the shop where you have your snapshots printed can do a blowup for you but, failing this, check the classified telephone directory for a source near you. The New York Yellow Pages list the service under Photo Copying, and I imagine this is the accepted designation anywhere within the United States. Photostatic enlargements are inexpensive and can often be done while you wait. Remember the process can reduce as well as expand and, if you find something in a book you'd like to reproduce in stitches, a copy can be made directly from the page without harming the volume in the least.

With blowup complete, I taped it to my drawing board. This is the moment to break out that masking tape you purchased. Just tear off small pieces and apply them, partly to the corners of the photostat, and partly to the drawing board. You'll find this method more practical than using drawing pins.

Over the photostat, I taped a sheet of tracing paper, then very carefully followed the outlines from whiskers to fish fins with my black, thin-line felt pen.

If you want to make changes in the original, now is the time. You may delete, or add, or alter to suit your purposes or your fancies. Look closely at the photograph (Fig. 3, after p. 32) and you'll see I made one departure from my model. The Indian painter had given his animal a somewhat attenuated look by flattening its back. For my pillow, I felt a rounder, plumper cat would compose better. The line change was first sketched in pencil on the tracing paper. When I was satisfied with the curve, the position of the spots was moved over to meet it (again in pencil) and the alterations were inked in with the rest of the body.

With photostat and tracing paper untaped from the board, it was time for the ultimate step. I laid a sheet of white paper on the drawing board and put the tracing paper over it. This is important because the white background makes the black lines stand out very clearly and they're easier to read through the canvas mesh. Over all this, I placed my canvas (already cut to size and hemmed. See Chapter I). This particular canvas, incidentally, is 10-count. Ordinarily I would find this mesh rather large to use for a pillow, but it suited the primitive quality and the broad color areas of the subject.

When more precise models are involved, I'm meticulous about matching meshes exactly to the lines of the drawing, but Cat is free and flexible so I only made certain the canvas threads followed the line of the longest straight sections in the somewhat erratic border. It's nearly always important to make some indication of mesh direction. If you don't, you'll find your subject creeping off on a bias you never intended and it won't get better as you go along. The defection will be more pronounced with each new row of stitches. The needle arbitrarily follows meshes, and the accurate right angle you drew (or thought you drew) can march resolutely away from the line you inked.

For this phase of the transferal, I suggest you use drawing pins to hold tracing and canvas firmly on the board. They're easier to move around when you're adjusting and readjusting canvas threads to inked-in outlines.

Now, with the gray felt pen, I drew directly on the canvas. Slowly and carefully because you will want only the simplest skeletal outline, the drawing underneath was duplicated, and Cat had advanced one more step.

With the small reproduction as reference, I selected the wools. The colors I chose pretty closely approximate those of the original, and the palette is limited. A wide range of graded shades would have been a terrible mistake for a traveling project. This is awfully good advice to keep in mind.

The stitches I used vary somewhat. The background is worked in herringbone stitch. This was the first time I ever used it—and the last. I find it slow and tricky. Cat herself and a good part of the fish are done in basketweave (page 43). The collar is a kind of bastard bargello for contrast. Because I wanted the fish to have some dimension, I chose the Smyrna stitch (page 58). Spotting and shading the fat crosses with tones of grayed mauve made him a plump catch.

Admittedly, I strayed from orthodox needlepoint techniques in this design example. I used an outline embroidery stitch in mercerized floss for the whiskers and spiny parts of the fish fins, but I felt this was a legitimate liberty. The idea was to duplicate the painting as closely as possible, and that would have been impossible within the strict boundaries of conventional needlepoint stitches. The outlines were simply embroidered *over* the completed basketweave stitch and the effect was exactly what I'd envisioned.

The addition of beads is really more Victorian hangover than modern departure. Caviar beads among the fish scales seemed appropriate, so I put them there. Having gone that far, bugle beads for the cat's eyes followed naturally.

So—there you have the long story of Cat, from head to tail; from inspiration to completed pillow.

Possibly you may feel the liberties I took with this project are frivolous and should, therefore, exclude it from the class of authentic and acceptable needlepoint. You may, of course, be correct but I can see no good reason why there should be firm, inflexible, unbreakable rules about conforming to pre-established methods or mores in any creative media (a category in which I definitely include needlepoint). Devices and inventions are often allowable, fresh and refreshing, so I invite you to feel free.

Fly (Fig. 4, after p. 32) is only a variation of the techniques used for Cat with Fish, but the differences are worth exploring because they present problems the cat design did not.

First of all, Fly is far more detailed, and his members infinitely more delicate.

Second, I wanted him to be a mirror image of himself. Since both halves were to be more or less equal, he couldn't be treated as casually as Cat.

Third, Fly is worked on finer, therefore less transparent canvas (14 count) and so was difficult to trace.

I can't tell you why the fly appealed to me as a subject. On the whole, I'm no fonder of flies than are most people. I believe it was the delicately intricate network of pattern, and the challenge of achieving a look of transparency in the wings with a dense, essentially opaque material that interested me.

The body of the fly in the original clipping measures approximately 2½ inches from tip of foreleg to tip of hind leg. It was blown up to 11½ inches which, for a fly, is pretty close to science fiction proportions.

This time I ruled a vertical line straight through the center of the photostat before I taped the tracing paper over it, and only one half of the fly was outlined with the black felt pen. When I removed the tracing paper, I folded it down the center, and simply retraced what I'd done on the blank half of the paper. When unfolded, I had the complete body of the fly, with one side exactly duplicating the other.

Following the center fold of the paper, I ruled a heavy pencil line vertically, then crossed it with a horizontal line—again through the center of the body. Since Fly was to sit directly in the middle of a cushion for a low bench, I then ruled the boundary lines for a 16-inch square, or the size of the seat. The identical measurement, and the center crossed lines were inked onto the canvas itself with the gray felt pen.

Everything was now ready for final transfer but, because of the density of the mesh, coupled with the complexity of the markings, the design proved impossible to read accurately when it was taped to the drawing board.

So—one bright morning—I taped the tracing paper to a window pane. I was ever so careful to match the crossed lines of the tracing to the crossed lines drawn on the canvas and, as I followed the outline underneath with the gray felt pen, I constantly checked and rechecked to make certain the threads hadn't shifted from the vertical and horizontal lines underneath. All this care made for slow progress but, if the tracing wasn't done with precision, the finished tapestry would lose all point.

An easier method here (certainly easier on the arms) would have been to tape tracing paper and canvas to a glass-topped table and set a lamp underneath, but not everybody owns a glass-topped table. Nearly everyone has a window.

Fly is worked in subtle, grayed tones which duplicate quite accurately those in the small illustration. Again, I constantly referred to the mounted clipping for changing shades and gradations.

The cushion is worked entirely in basketweave stitch. The grids of the background screen were counted off from the original center lines after the tracing was finished. The crossbars were done first, and the spaces between filled in afterward.

This same photostat-transfer method was used for the small shell pillows but the blowup step was left out for the bird's nest (Fig. 5, after p. 32). Because the nest in the jewelry advertisement was the size I wanted it to be in the first place, I simply made my tracing from the photograph. The eggs that replace the gems were sketched in pencil and, when the arrangement pleased me, the outlines were inked in. In fact, I used three hens eggs as models so I could duplicate the shadows and highlights as closely as it's possible in wool stitches.

Photostat of two shell motifs to be transferred to canvas to make two small shell pillows.

YOUR OWN DESIGNS

Ways of making use of the photostat-trace-transfer method are varied and elastic. It isn't even necessary to enlarge just one single object. You can do a *decoupage* or paste-up composition of flowers, fruit, vegetables or creatures. You can include caterpillars and beetles in a flower still life, and flutter butterflies or birds over the production. The limit is the boundary of your imagination.

Seed catalogs are splendid sources with their clean, no-nonsense illustrations of the very best of growing things. These are readily available.

For fanciful effects, always keep an eye open for interesting subjects to clip from magazines you're about to discard. Eventually you'll build up a sort of savings bank of ideas and possibilities. Just don't attempt to create something inspired on impulse, or from inappropriate, out-of-scale material. Make this a project that grows over a period of time. You'll soon train yourself to recognize possibilities and judge potentials. Don't forget that the scale and proportion of each individual element should be consistent. The combination of a 3-inch buttercup, a 2-inch rose and a ½-inch robin pasted together in a group are going to look pretty silly. What doesn't matter is whether or not the cutouts are in color. You can mix them up because the photostat will be in black and white anyway.

As in true decoupage, the system involves cutting around the outline of each illustration. Shift the components around on a blank sheet of paper until the composition pleases you. Only then, paste the assemblage permanently on paper. Decide what size you want the enlargement, mark the dimensions clearly and trot off to the photostat establishment.

When the blowup is completed, you will simply proceed with your line drawing on tracing paper and subsequent transfer to canvas.

The original design is a decoupage of a dragonfly, lizard and grasses.

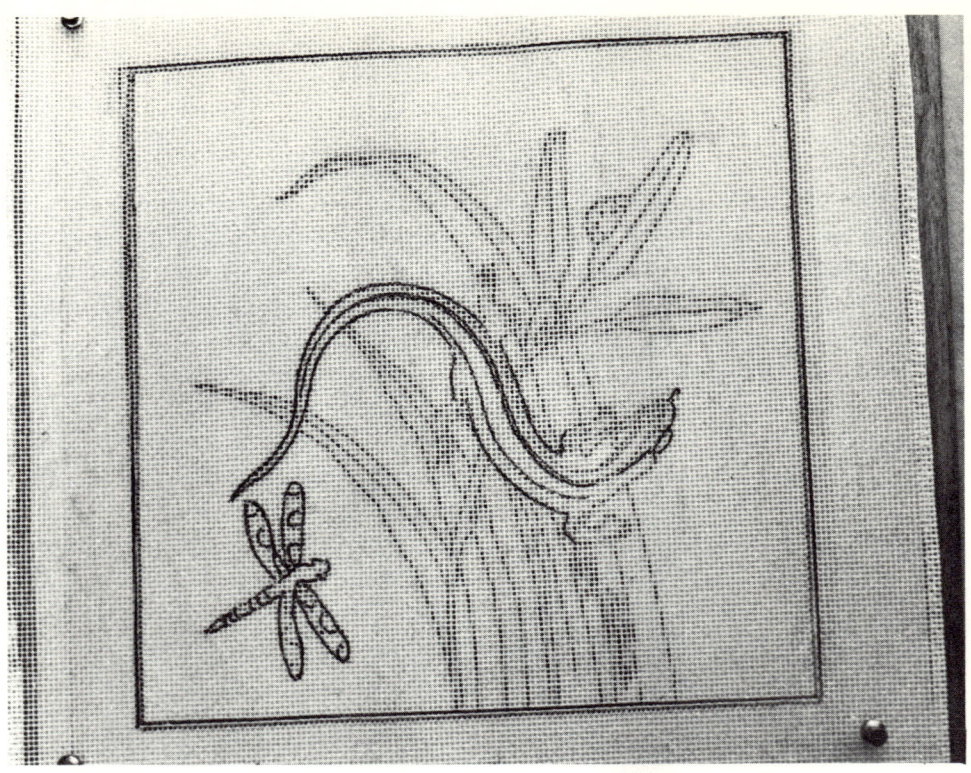

Outlining the design with a felt-tip pen onto the canvas which is overlayed on the tracing of the photostat.

To design a rug

There are good, sound ways of using the photostat and tracing system for rugs as well as for smaller pieces but, faced with an increased area, your transfer process will be somewhat different. It will take considerably more planning and scheming than you're apt to devote to a 14-inch square pillow.

Some years ago I clipped and saved a how-to magazine article about needlepoint rugs. It suggested the adaptation of a fabric or wallpaper pattern, and instructed the reader to place a piece of tracing paper over the motif of her choice, then make an outline drawing with a felt-tipped pen.

So far it's the familiar story, but it went on to say, "Now place your rug canvas on top of the drawing and trace the design right on the canvas with a felt pen." End of lesson.

To this day I have a cartoon-like vision of a woman holding a 40- by 60-inch canvas in one hand and a neat tracing of a 5- or 6-inch floral cluster in the other. In my mental picture, the lady wears an extremely puzzled expression.

A rug is a big investment in time, labor, wool, canvas and true devotion. It's going to require quite a lot more careful consideration and preparation than the above instructions for instant-rug indicate.

Before you make that tracing, it's a good idea to make several decisions. You've probably determined the size of the rug and whether you will do it in one piece or in sections. Now you must think about distribution and about whether you want a border that's meaningful or nearly non-existent. It can be a simple frame for what goes on inside or, literally, it can be the whole show.

The most helpful device to use for arriving at these primary decisions about borders and placement of design elements is to make several small, scaled-to-measure outlines of your rug. Allowing 1 inch on your ruler to equal 1 foot, draw a series of rectangles on scrap paper. If, for example, you have a 3- by 5-foot rug in mind, prepare a bunch of little 3- by 5-inch blanks. Play around with these. Just doodle to get an idea of composition, arrangement and spacing. The trial runs will make up your mind about whether you want your design scattered, formal tight or asymmetrically fancy free. See Chapter V.

This method will also help you decide the size of your finished motifs. Remember that if a roughly indicated flower measures ½ inch on your sketch, it will be a 6-inch blossom in real-life stitches, while a ¼-inch leaf will actually be 3 inches long.

When you have the picture as a whole on paper as well as in your head and are quite content with the composition, *that's* the time to make a tracing. Before you place your canvas over it you'll doubtless want the tracing blown up to another dimension besides. Your preliminary scribbles will have determined the eventual size. If you're repeating only one motif from that fabric or wallpaper pattern, you'll now know how best to arrange it in true scale. If you've decided on a combination of several elements, their proportions and placement will also have been predetermined by those working sketches.

Designing a rug isn't an impossible undertaking. It's just a little more complex than that magazine article might lead you to believe.

Perhaps the rug designs on the next page might interest you.

The first is a tightly formal, rather traditional cluster of flowers found in a chintz. Some of the tracings should be blown up to a larger scale than others so the grouping won't look like a flower salad.

The border is a suggested single garland of the smallest of the flowers, and their leaves. In the fabric, these blossoms are an intense blue.

The second scatters the flowers as though they'd been gathered in a basket, then casually tossed onto the rug. Arrange and rearrange your tracings of the enlargements. Anything which *seems* as careless as this composition, will often require more planning than a totally stylized arrangement.

For a border, the wild abandon inside seems to need the control of an orderly enclosure, like the suggested folded ribbon bands.

The third design is all border. The design makes full use of the branches that sprawl across the chintz to trail off into little tendrils and budlets.

This design should be kept free and loose. Don't attempt to match side for side; corner for corner, or the effect will be set and rigid. Simply distribute color values and flower proportions so that balance is achieved with no loss of flow.

Quite honestly, for anything as large and hopefully enduring as a floor cover-

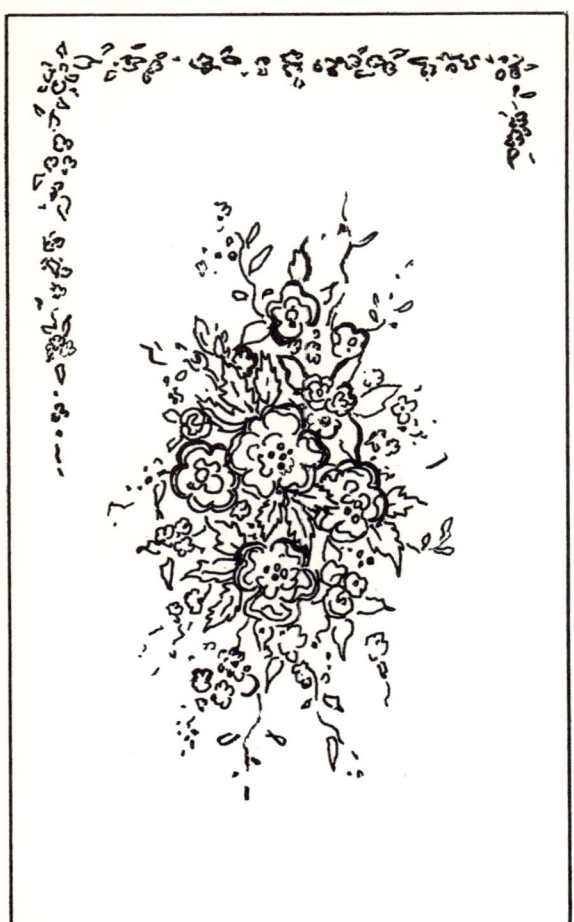

Wilhelmina Feiner's possible designs for needlepoint rugs.

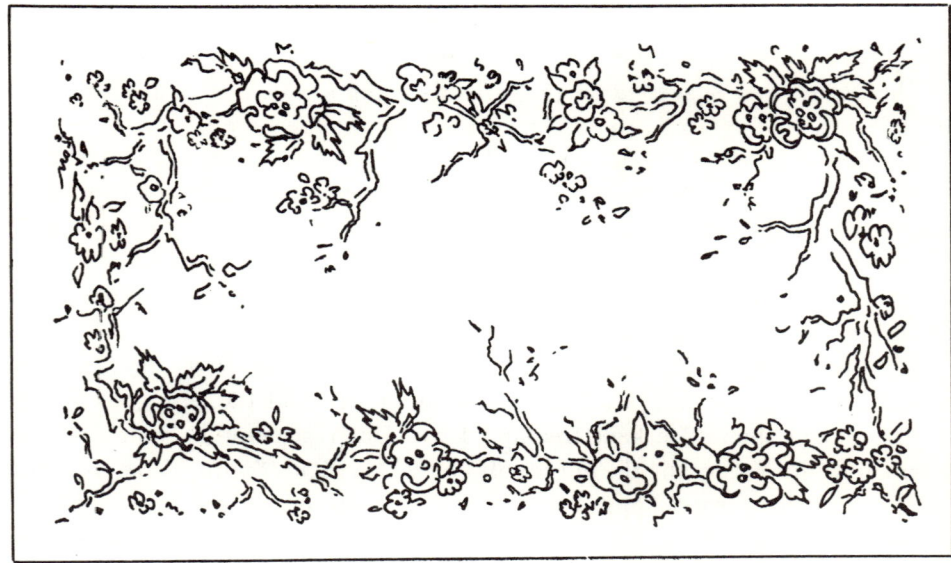

ing, I should prefer to tie my design into something less transient than a fabric or wallpaper. These rarely are forever, whereas a rug, like a diamond, almost is. I want to feel I haven't put my soul into a project that will soon represent only the fading memory of some long-gone chintz. Reserve this form of design cribbing for a few pillows or, at most, a couple of chair seats.

Try using other sources of inspiration. An antique platter, for instance, or the elaborate marquetry geometrics of an inlaid box could be translated into a wonderfully handsome small rug. Should this sort of adaptation tax your designing abilities, then find a fabulous color plate in a book or a magazine which might be blown up to accommodate itself to rug size.

The remarkable thing is, you'll find yourself looking at almost anything and everything with a needlepointer's selective eye and equating it in needlepoint terms. As you can see, this is a general case in point for that clipping folder. If an idea can be snipped, file it for the future. If it can't, make a note instead so you'll know what it is, and where it can be found when you want it. For example, there's an endearing oriental frog on a certain page in a certain art publication I want to keep intact. It may be a year or more before I'm inspired to start stitching the creature but, when the day comes, I won't tear the bookcases apart looking for him.

Design Method 2

This system employs the transfer-trace formula used in all the examples described in Design Method 1, and it's often helpful where large areas are involved. The difference lies in the elimination of the photostatic enlargement.

The photo copying machine can blow up only to a limited size. Beyond this, you have a problem. One way out is to woo an amiable photostatter, who will enlarge your model in sections. The pieces can be pasted together and you'll carry on from there. Given the amiable photostatter, this method works but, when I'm confronted with a really mammoth project, I find the classic copying-by-squares or grid method is a happier solution. If your subject isn't too complex, and you're willing to check and recheck measurements, you should be able to bring it off even though you may have very little ability to draw—or, none at all.

The animal tapestry (Fig. 6, after p. 32) is a product of this procedure and, because the components themselves are blocked in so simply, it wasn't a difficult job to do.

The panel is copied from the reproduction of a Chinese cut-paper panel; the traditional New Year's decoration made by peasants in most of the provinces of Central China. These vibrantly colored, childlike but sophisticated inspirations are pasted to the oiled paper substitute for window glass.

I've no clue to the size of the original window, but the reproduction is only a fraction more than 10 inches by a little less than $5\frac{3}{4}$. The needlepoint hanging measures 5 feet 3 inches by 3 feet; a dramatic enlargement that would have required a fairly large number of pasted-together photostats.

Transferral of the design by the copy-by-squares or grid method. Shown here is the tracing of the original design and the enlargement.

To begin, I placed a sheet of tracing paper over the small reproduction and carefully followed the outline of each animal and branch with a very sharp pencil. Next, I divided the tracing into squares as shown. If the model of your choice isn't worth preserving, you can omit the tracing process and draw your squares directly on it. My illustration is the frontispiece for a handsome book which I certainly didn't want to damage.

Now I was ready to expand. With transparent tape I joined four sheets of blank newsprint as neatly as possible and drew my outer dimensions. The area was then divided into 1-foot squares—fifteen of them, plus three 1-foot by 3-inch rectangles at the bottom. Both outline and squared divisions were inked in with the black felt pen because I wanted them to stay with me through the countless erasures I knew I'd be making.

Because the squares drawn on the little tracing measure 1¾ inches, and a scale ruler stops at 1½ inches, I made my own scale by dividing the 1¾ inches into twelve parts. In the end, I found this scrap of paper more maneuverable than a real ruler anyway.

I'm blessed with space for a large work table but, if you're not so fortunate, the dining room table (protected) will do just as well or, if you're agile, the floor.

With my taped-together, squared-off newsprint, the small tracing, my made-up ruler and a real one spread out before me, I began work with a large, soft pencil: checking, sketching, comparing, erasing and—erasing. If the end of the purple pig's snout on the tracing measured 5½ inches from the right-hand corner of the lower middle square, and a bit more than 1 inch from the bottom on my false ruler, that's where it is, in real-life inches, on the enlargement. Constantly checking points along the way, then joining them with penciled lines, I plowed on to the tips of the bull's horns in the upper left-hand square to complete the magnified version.

It's not important for this pencil drawing to be fastidiously neat and clean. Your false moves needn't be erased to invisibility because, when you've achieved the final shape and position of the elements and objects, you'll go over these with the black felt pen. The black outline is what you'll see through the canvas meshes, not the penciled errors and false starts, and the tracing process will be exactly the same as described for Cat with Fish and Fly. In other words, it's the identical procedure highly magnified and, happily, it's less confusing to accomplish than it is to read.

The hanging is worked on 12-count mono canvas, entirely in basketweave stitch. As usual, the little color reproduction was constantly referred to for color changes, shadings and accents.

If all this sounds Herculean, it really isn't. Like a rug, the tapestry will be around for years and years. It took some months to complete (eight, if you'd really like to know), and the canvas ate a good deal of wool (about six pounds). Compared to these cold facts and figures, the relatively short time devoted to the initial steps seems quite inconsequential.

Design Method 3

This one is a sort of fooling-around technique and, if you like plain geometry, bold colors and direct statements, it's one with enough potential possibilities to keep you in ideas for a good long while.

To arrive at your design, I suggest you do the fooling around on graph paper. The lines will correspond to the canvas meshes so the pattern you form will come out in stitches exactly as it looks on paper.

Figures 7 and 8 after p. 32 illustrate steps from crisscrossed pencil lines to finished needlepoint pillow. The design becomes purely a progression of squares, and triangles arrived at by erasing some of the lines and retaining others. Only one was moved from the original maze—the orange square, along with the gold and green areas above it. This line was lowered about a half inch in order to achieve what I like to believe is a bit of painterly asymmetry.

For a project of this sort it's always a good idea to make a finished cartoon to act as guide to color as well as placement. This particular trial sketch indicates not only color selections, but the types of stitches I planned to use as well. It was to be (and is) an experiment in texture as well as pattern and color. Thus, the orange square is worked in Scotch stitch, the green areas in brick stitch, the terra cotta in cross-stitch (a very slow one I don't much recommend for general use, by the way), and the white sections in basketweave. The gold and deep brown are both done in Gobelin stitch; the first over two threads, the other over only one. A design can be adapted from nothing more complicated than a series of squares or diagonals.

All these basic concepts are likely to send out messages you can translate into your own terms. Starting with one prototype, dozens of combinations can happen and, as a group of pillows, they could be exceedingly stylish flung together on a large sofa. By adding one color, subtracting another, and mixing each combination a little differently, you'll come up with a wonderfully dizzy needlepoint kaleidoscope.

Painting your canvas

Because the needlepoint methods to follow must never be painted on canvas, this seems the moment to discuss the process as it relates to the preceding techniques.

As I stated earlier in this chapter, I don't entirely approve of applying paint to canvas. I don't like being kept rigidly within the bounds of any area. Once a section has been shaped and shaded into one unalterable curve or color, I feel dictated to. Even if it's I who's done the dictating, I resent it. However, if you honestly feel you need such a crutch, this is the way to go about building it.

In addition to the materials listed on page 22, you will purchase jars or tubes of acrylic paints and several good brushes. It's a good idea to put your canvas on a clean sheet of white blotting paper before you begin to paint, so add this to your shopping list.

When your basic outline has been drawn in, make certain you have a color guide to follow. If you're copying something, have it at hand. If it's an original, plot your colors on paper before you touch brush to canvas. Remember that what you do now is irrevocable. You can't rip out paint as you can stitches later on.

Your paints should be thinned with water to the consistency of light cream. In this runny state, it's practical to mix the colors in small cups or jars.

Don't put too much paint on your brush. You must keep the colors neatly within the outlines and, if the brush is too wet, the paint will inevitably creep beyond the boundaries you've determined. It's also important for the color to stay on the top side of the canvas. Don't let it bleed through to the back, and don't clog the pores.

Oil paints, plus turpentine and a drying medium can be substituted for the acrylics, but I don't advise them. They're messier to work with, smellier and take days to dry before you can put needle to canvas.

Design Method 4

This sections deals with the Florentine family, flame variations and any other stitches which, by count alone, progress over an empty canvas.

Aside from the almost inevitable crossed center lines, if you do mark any guides, they'll only whisper their message.

The first project I ever attempted without having made and transferred a design is pictured in (Fig. 9, after p. 64). Blindly and blithely, I stepped right

FIGURE 1 The mark of the author, a W surmounting back-to-back Fs, all enclosed within a box to distinguish it from the design of the piece.

FIGURE 2 Cat with Fish.

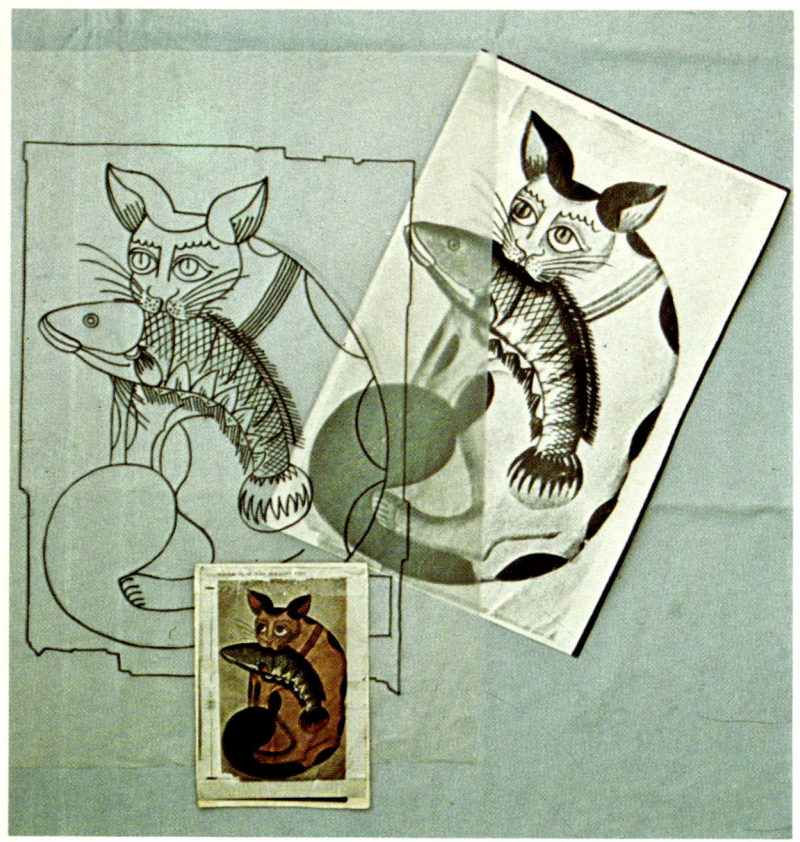

FIGURE 3 Cat with Fish: photostat, original color reproduction and tracing.

FIGURE 4 The finished needlepoint fly compared to the original color photo.

FIGURE 5 The original photo of the bird's nest was the right size for the pillow. Therefore the step of blowing up the original design could be eliminated. The tracing could be made directly from the original design.

FIGURE 6 Because of the complexity and size of the design, this animal tapestry had to be enlarged by means of the grid method (design method #2).

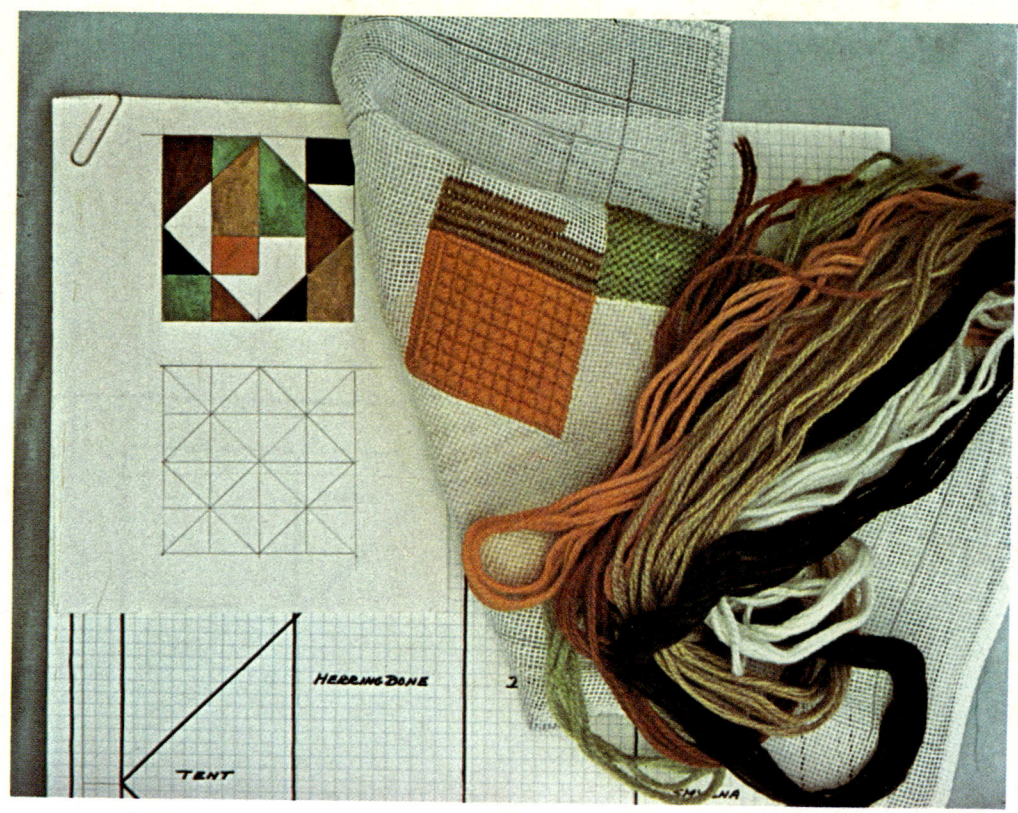

FIGURE 7 The design can be worked out on graph paper first and then a sampler of stitches can be made, color-coding the yarn and particular stitch to the color sketch of the pillow.

FIGURE 8 Finished pillow.

YOUR OWN DESIGNS 37

into a blank, uncharted canvas and the problems ahead didn't trouble me at all. The idea was clear inside my skull, but putting it into stitches was something else again. There was a good deal of patient (more or less) picking out to be done before I faced the fact that my difficulties were as much concerned with simple arithmetic as they were with needlepoint. I realized, too, that if the count were off by so much as a single mesh, the whole plan would fall apart and I'd have nothing but an amateurish botch to show for all my stitches.

This initial experiment hasn't anything to do with the Florentines and, though it may have been done countless times before, I've never seen or read about it—not in any book, nor in any example of needlepoint I've come upon—so I like to delude myself into believing it's my own invention born of necessity.

When the idea of doing an all-over needlepoint repeat for a small Biedermeier bench occurred to me, I was scarcely aware of the word bargello, and Florentines were people who lived happily in Florence. Had I known how to do these stitches, I shouldn't have stumbled on the method I used. Since I like it, that would have been a pity.

Basket weave was the only stitch I knew how to do for the body of any piece, so I made it travel in four directions instead of one to form the square patterns. These I joined together with smaller squares done in the rather dimensional triangle stitch (page 60). The surface is bordered with rows of Smyrna stitch (page 58), and the boxing is a smooth, one-tone basket weave to contrast with the almost jewellike look of the top section.

Because I could track down no gimp or trim that looked at all well with my

Detailed look at the stitches of this project: the basket weave, triangle stitch and Smyrna stitch.

wool colors, I braided several shades of the yarn together to finish off the final upholstery. Remember this trick. It's not difficult to do and, all too often, the perfect commercial edging simply doesn't exist.

The bench covering was made on 14-count canvas, but I've always felt it would be just as effective to duplicate the design on a much coarser mesh.

I used crewel wool for this project and I suspect it has a large quantity of Siamese fur woven into it for strength. One of my cats decided I was making the piece expressly for him and managed to nest in it during non-needlepointing hours. In its finished state, the bench is still Irving's favorite throne.

Of course I did, eventually, learn the Florentine-bargello stitches, and I find them extraordinarily adaptable and useful in all the forms described in Chapter III.

The chair seat (Fig. 10, after p. 64) is done in one of them. This is the Gobelin stitch worked over two meshes of 12-count mono canvas. The result is a fat, ropy texture, which is becoming to the sturdy little Biedermeier chair it upholsters.

The pictured chair is one of four. The first served as a model for the remaining three. They took time, but almost no thought at all.

For these seats, the crossed center lines were widened to become part of the design itself. The dimensions of the center motif were only lightly indicated on the canvas. The actual design was established on graph paper with color notes roughly painted in.

The crossed bands were stitched first, then the simple center square. After that, it was a matter of counting and following the graph.

Please believe my admonitions about not drawing geometrics too definitely on canvas. You'll be tempted to follow them exactly, and they'll almost never be accurate enough. The inked-in angle that *seems* to slant in the proper direction can turn mean and willful. You'll find line and stitches have parted company and nothing in this world will ever reunite them—short of picking out and starting over, of course. So, count as you progress. The angles and right angles will prove themselves numerically and arithmetically.

All this may sound something of a bore, but it's really rather satisfying and you'll find it quickly becomes an automatic procedure.

I should imagine the woven ribbon design on the chair shown in Fig. 11 after p. 64 has been done for about as long as needlepoint itself has been around. Though it's totally traditional, it can be as modern and fresh as the colors you choose. The size of the stitches and the width of the ribbon can be varied infinitely. It's effective in anything from the finest petit point to a large mesh rug canvas. In fact, I plan to repeat it one day in the brightest and clearest of classic Roman stripe colors on a small rug. Straight rows of ribbons, mitered at the corners, will be the border.

The stitch used here in Florentine. The canvas mesh is 12-count, and the wool was worked over two threads (one mesh).

YOUR OWN DESIGNS

Flame patterns and what can be done with them are pretty well covered in Chapter III, but you might like to have a try at an abstract version.

The pillow (Fig. 12, after p. 64) throws every rule right out the window but, essentially, it's still flame stitch. Wild and free as this berserk bargello may appear, it's still a good idea to plot the direction of the color sweeps and gradations on paper. Keeping in mind the axiom that nothing is as easy as it looks, indicate the shapes of the areas lightly on the canvas so the swoops and swirls won't turn stiff and awkward.

Stay loose when you make these sketches and do them quickly so they won't look forced on contrived. Used your water colors and a brush. Let the colors flow together if they will and you can blend your wools almost as freely. Make a number of these trials (some of them will be terrible) until you have one you really like well enough to want to reproduce in stitches.

Any number of versions can be worked out; none will repeat, and the textures you create will be astonishingly varied too.

With all these methods, instructions and suggestions to boost you into becoming your own skilled designer, you've now only to master the stitches. Once you understand them and realize their possibilities (and their limitations as well), you can make them interpret just about any idea that may jump into your head.

One discovery will lead to another. One experiment will surprise you into an entire series of creative combinations and conceptions. You'll find yourself with more marvelous ideas you'd like to translate into stitches than your fingers can ever find time to execute. Ready-made, predesigned canvases will be in the shops for someone else to buy. Blank, virgin canvas is for you—you'll have your own drawings to fill in.

III

All about Stitches

All about stitches

More accurately, the title of this chapter should read, "All about *Some* Stitches," for there are several hundred varieties and variations I never wish to master. Barring whatever technical challenge they may offer, for me these stitches serve no purpose other than to snarl my wool and stretch my canvas into bizarre shapes.

I've experimented with the intricacies of tramé, the triple leviathan, the encroaching Gobelin and the long-armed cross-stitch among others, and have promptly struck them from my repertoire of stitchery. Aside from their rather jolly names, I don't honestly think they have much to recommend them to the average modern needlepointer.

Certain of the off-beat stitches I do find helpful. They can be decorative, diverting and texturally interesting. I use them from time to time to carry out specific design ideas, and I suggest you try them in special areas. You'll find diagrams and descriptions at the end of the list of more generally serviceable stitches.

Threading your needle

Before you learn any stitch, you must know how to thread a needle with wool. Don't attempt to slip an end of yarn directly through the needle's eye as you would do with ordinary sewing thread. It won't work. Instead, follow these steps.

1) Hold needle in your left hand, and the yarn in your right. Make a loop of the wool (leaving one end short; the other long). With thumb and forefinger, pinch loop tightly over flat side of the eye. Hold it as closely and firmly as you can. (top, left)

42 ADVENTURE IN NEEDLEPOINT

Steps in threading the needle.

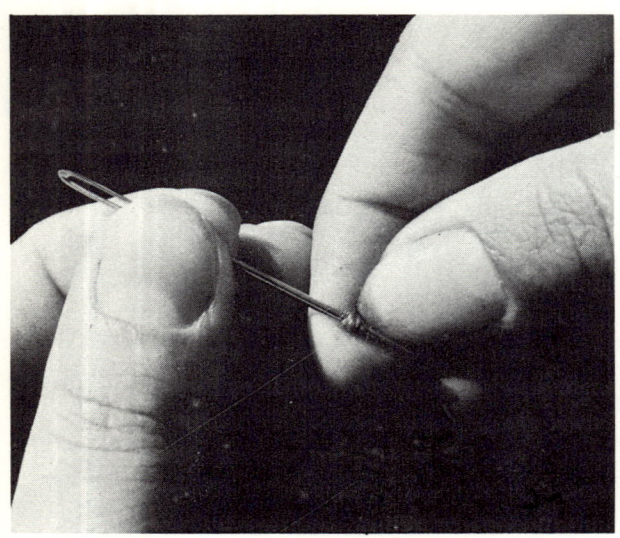
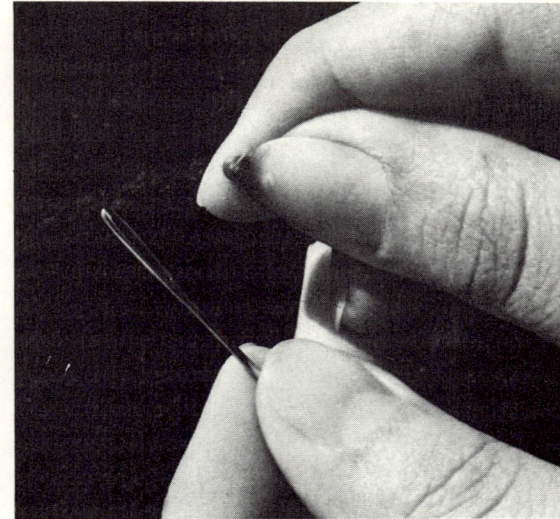
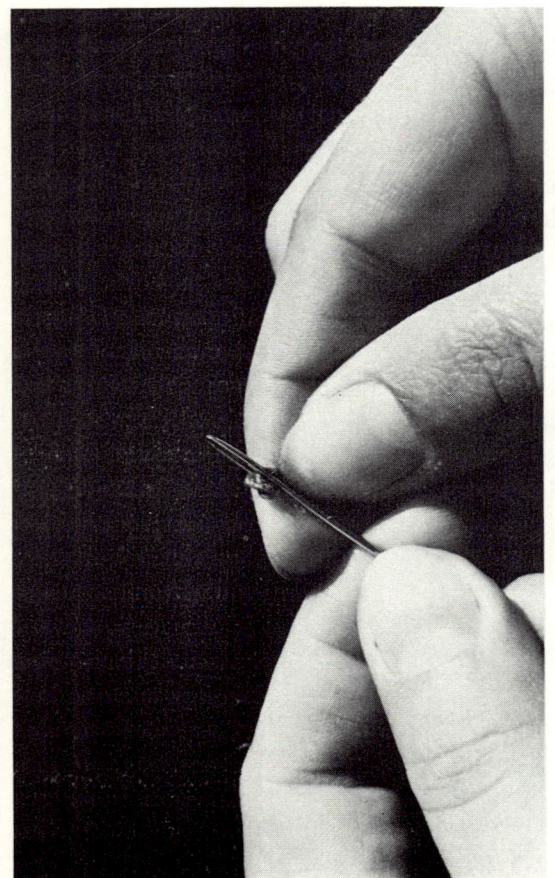
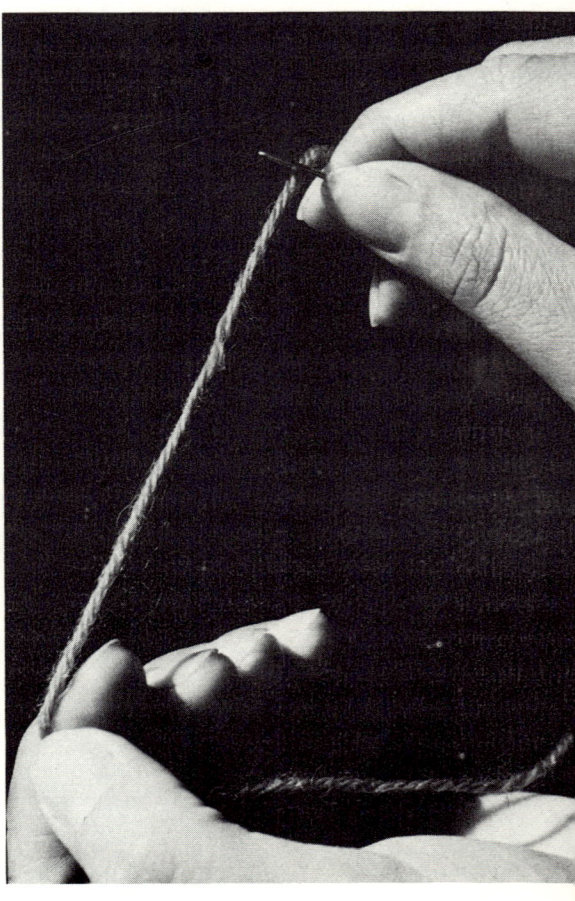

ALL ABOUT STITCHES 43

2) Without relaxing your grip on the doubled-up yarn, zip it downward over the length of the needle. (top, right)
3) Continue to pinch the yarn loop hard as you feed it into the needle's eye. The wool will have flattened and fanned out slightly. All plies will pass through evenly and smoothly. (bottom, left)
4) Release your hold and ease the yarn through until the shorter end passes the eye and the loop is eliminated. (bottom, right)

If this seems at all complicated, it isn't. As in a film clip, these separately illustrated steps are really only one speedy, uncomplicated motion.

Now—make a neat knot at the longer end of your strand, and we'll begin a lesson in stitches.

The basket-weave stitch

For a vast majority of needlepointers the catalog of stitches begins with this one, then comes to an abrupt and conclusive end. Although I don't agree that it's the one and absolutely only, there's no doubt about the fact that basket weave fills more requirements (and canvases) than any other stitch.

The list of its merits is long. It's functional, adaptable and doesn't pull the canvas out of shape as many other stitches do. It can be used both for mono canvas and Penelope; for stitches large, or very small. It's smooth on the front side, has a firm, durable backside, and is fleet and fun to do. For a sleek, unbroken look don't fool around—use it consistently all over your canvas, even in the smallest design areas.

This stitch is called, alternately, the *bias tent* and the *diagonal*, but it's most often referred to as *basket weave*. A look at the reverse side will tell you why.

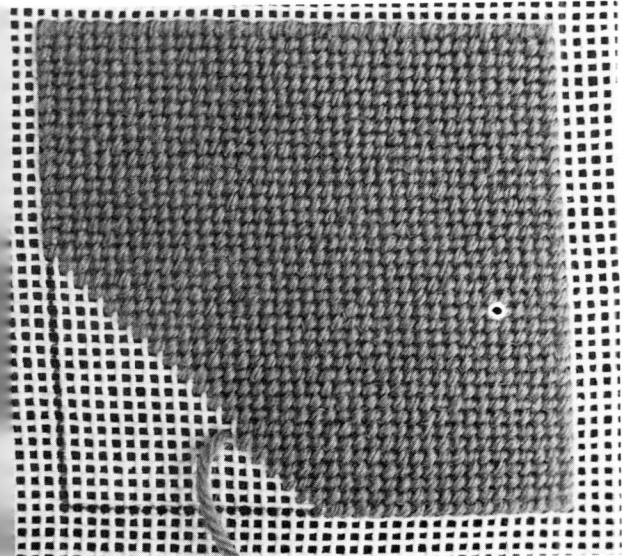

Basket weave (front).

Basket weave (back).

44 ADVENTURE IN NEEDLEPOINT

Admittedly, the ideal method to follow in learning a stitch is to have a private teacher at your elbow as you take those first, tentative pokes with the needle. When you've been led from mesh to mesh, encouraged, scolded, shown where you've gone wrong and been ordered to take out what you've put in a few times, the process soon becomes automatic and you're an instantly independent needlepointer.

I can only guide you in spirit and by chart and, since I know many people either go to pieces, or simply draw a blank at the sight of a diagram, I'll try to be as kindergarten explicit as possible. Those among you who are lightening-quick studies, bear with us, please—but, no matter how eptly clever, you'll surely have to pick out a certain number of stitches, so practice on a scrap of canvas until you're quite, quite sure of yourself.

To begin the basket weave, take your threaded needle in hand and insert it from the *front* side of your canvas, an inch or more away from the *upper right-hand corner* of the outermost limit you've indicated for your background area. Draw the needle up, from back to front, through mesh #1, then down through mesh #2. Note that your knot will remain perched on the right side of the canvas.

This first, lonely stitch is the apex of a triangle you'll begin to form. The next step will be to bring your needle up, from back to front of canvas, through mesh #3 (to the left of #1), and down again through mesh #4 (to the left of #2). You have now laid two slanting stitches side by side.

Next, bring your needle up through mesh #5 (just below and to the right of #1). Return the needle downward, through #6 (below and to the right of #2). You have three slanting stitches which, as predicted, form a triangle.

The step to follow will be to bring the needle to the front of the canvas, through #7 (below #5).

Steps in the basket-weave stitch.

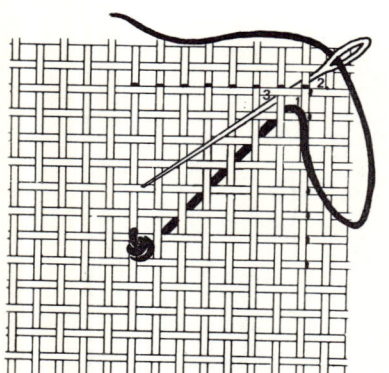 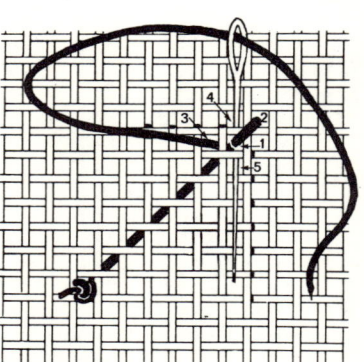 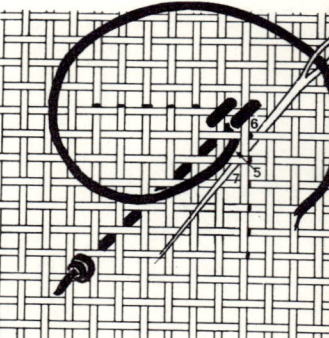

You're now ready to begin interlocking. The diagram shows you how to direct your needle. Through #8, under two canvas threads, and out through #9.

Draw the needle through, and insert it in mesh #1 (right under your very first stitch), but don't draw it through. Direct your needle to mesh #10—again under two canvas threads.

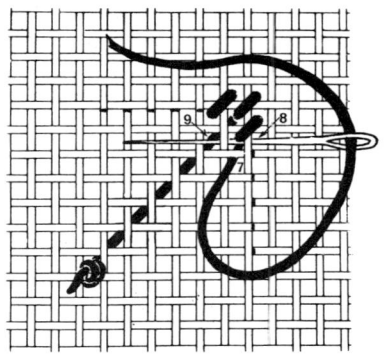 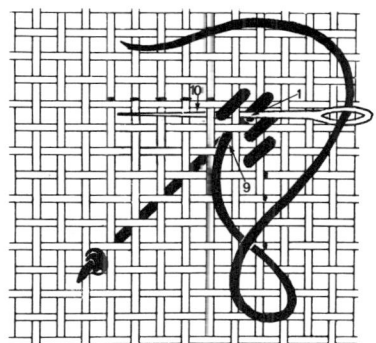 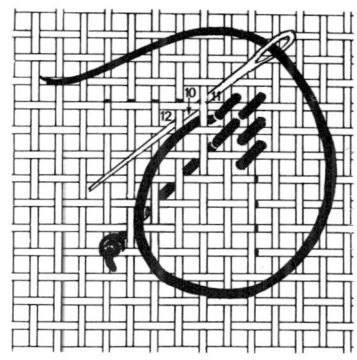

Pull your thread through and insert the needle as shown, through #11 (next to your second stitch). Direct it downward and on a slant to mesh #12.

Pull your thread through. Observe—your little triangle has grown.

Lay your fourth slanting stitch along the top boundary, next to the three you've already made. As you direct your needle downward, you should begin to realize that you've been here before. You're simply repeating the same operation, but with an increasing number of stitches. You'll build them, stitch on stitch, in an ever-widening diagonal line. Remember, always, to go under two canvas threads in a downward direction when you travel down—under two threads in a crosswise direction when you reverse and climb back up the diagonal.

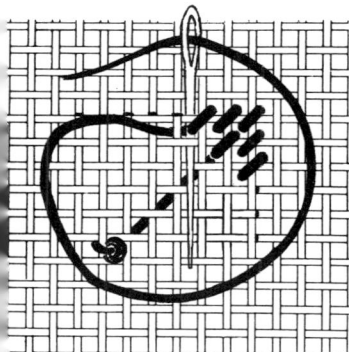 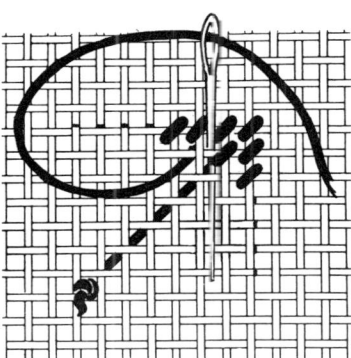 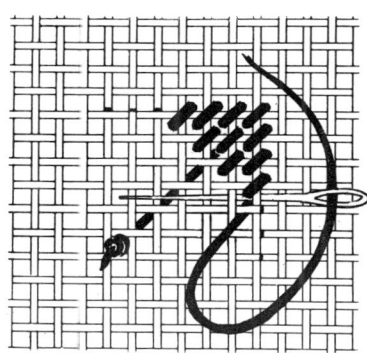

Possibly, instinct will tell you to turn your canvas as you change your stitch direction. Pay no attention to it. *You will always hold your canvas in a stationary position for the basket weave.* There will be one small, allowable exception to this rigid rule, but we'll come to that later on.

When you've completed eight or nine stitches horizontally and vertically on your practice triangle, you will have approached the knot you left on the surface of the canvas. Whack it off with your scissors. Its purpose was to hold the short length of yarn while you stitched over it on the back. Mission has been accomplished. It's permanently anchored.

As you reach the last inches (about three) of the strand you're using, the time has come to finish it off. Instead of bringing your needle back to the surface of the canvas, let it pass through to the back and neatly weave the wool over and under the finished stitches for about an inch. Snip off the short, remaining end.

To begin the next strand, weave it, too, into the stitches underneath (toward the spot where you left off). If you'll turn back to the photograph on page 43 showing the reverse side you'll see how the yarn ends have been woven in and clipped.

Bring the needle to the front through the mesh next to the last stitch you made. Continue the row as though there'd been no break. Incidentally, it's much better to end a thread and begin a new one *past* the edges or they'll look lumpy. You probably won't use the knot trick again until you start a new project. It's for beginnings only, when there's no other anchorage in sight.

* * *

Although there's a bit of a knack to learning basket weave, you can see it isn't at all difficult. Now that you're master, it will become not at all unpleasantly mechanical. The stitches build and grow, one locking into another, in a most satisfying and smoothly satisfactory manner, your canvas to fill and your ideas to interpret. This is a sturdily practical stitch but, at the same time, its flexibility allows you an amazing degree of creative freedom and inventiveness.

Basket weave may not be *the* stitch, but it's an awfully important and vital word in the needlepoint vocabulary.

A word to the left-handed

Because I am right-handed, the preceding instructions, as well as all those to follow, are plotted for the right-handed majority. As they are presented, the directions will only confuse the left-handed. Happily, all is not lost. If you turn the book upside down, you will find the diagrammed needle is now headed in your direction. For you, the upper right-hand corner will become the lower left and each step will be in reverse.

Some handy thoughts about basket weave

Use the reverse side of your basket weave stitches to "proof" your work as you go along. Mistakes will show up more plainly on the back than on the front. If you've broken that neat, even weave, you've broken some rule, so keep an eye on where you've been.

You must always reverse directions as you work. If you don't, an unattractive line that looks something like a zipper will form on the back, and a distinct ridge will appear on the front that no amount of wetting, blocking or pressing will ever remove.

If you've interrupted your stitching after finishing and securing a strand, always check back before you begin again. Search out the spot where you battened down your yarn so you'll take up from that last stitch and proceed in the proper direction.

A zipper-like stitch results if you do not reverse the direction of the canvas as you work.

It's all too easy to go blithely ahead without immediately being aware of your error. If you discover it after you've gone a number of rows beyond on a long, diagonal stretch, the picking out isn't going to be exactly larky.

A good little trick is to leave the last yarn end flying free, uncut and on the right side of your canvas. It will serve as a warning marker. This tip will be especially helpful if you're working on a large project and find yourself skipping from area to area.

When you do basket weave, you'll nearly always begin to work at, or near, the center of your design, rather than in the corner of the background.

This is not to say you won't follow all those preceding directions to the diagrammed letter. Begin stitching your background exactly as you've been taught—when the time comes. Start with the central motif and finish it first. After you've done that, you'll work your background toward the design and, eventually, surround it. Never stitch the background around a drawn-in outline. The design will lose all definition if you do.

As you begin in center field, make absolutely certain that your stitches are slanted in the proper direction—*up* toward the upper right-hand corner (where you'll launch into your background); *down* toward lower left.

If, alas, you discover much too late that you've pointed all those beautiful stitches in the wrong direction, (NW. by SE. instead of NE. by SW.), you can create a false starting point by turning your canvas so that either the lower right or the upper left corners are in the upper right position. This isn't an ideal solution but, when you're well into some inspired creation before you catch the mistake, it's the only way—short of picking out everything you've put in, that is. Such misadventures have overtaken me more than once, and I've gotten myself out of the miserable corners in just this way, but it's better to avoid the crisis in the first place.

That allowable instance when you may turn your canvas while work is in progress occurs when you're deeply involved with small, oddly shaped or intricately shaded details of your design. It will often seem more natural and, certainly, more convenient to attack these sections from the most accessible angle you can find. Hold the canvas in whatever position seems most comfortable. Any ridges you make on the back aren't going to show in such tiny areas. Just be careful to slant the stitches in the direction the surrounding stitches are pointed.

Try for an especially even tension when you're doing basket weave. Not only will your canvas stay obediently in shape, you'll find no white meshes winking through.

The continental stitch

The continental (sometimes referred to as the tent stitch) is closely related to the basket weave. In fact, if you look back at the basket weave photos (back and front), you'll be hard-pressed to see the difference between the two—from the front. The flip side is something else again.

Hard-core needlepoint traditionalists continue to use this stitch for filling in backgrounds as well as for all design areas but, though the continental has

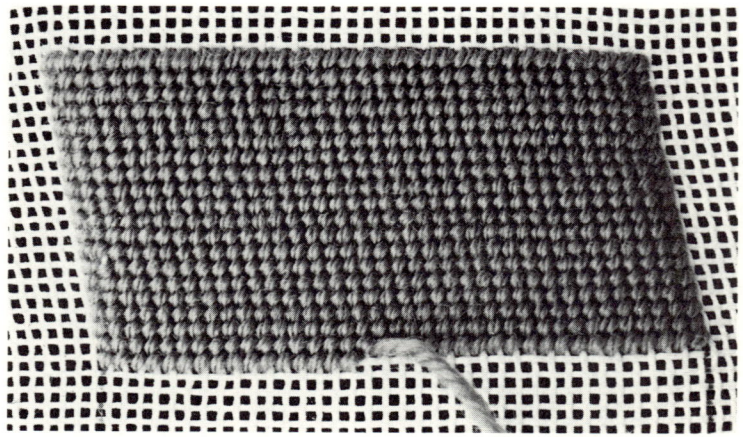

Continental stitch (front).

Continental stitch (back).

virtues, you'll find most modern stitchers don't think it's very practical for covering large sections of canvas.

There are several reasons for its having been cast aside; not the least is that it pulls the canvas into the most capriciously lopsided shapes you can imagine. In addition, it doesn't work up nearly as smoothly as basket weave, nor does it advance with that same easy, rythmic flow. In order to do the continental, you must swing your canvas entirely around at the end of every row and start back again in the opposite direction. In other words, each new line of stitches is worked from right to left, and there's no doubling back.

Place the knotted end of your strand of yarn on what will be your first stitch line. Start from the right, as indicated, and bring your needle to the front side through mesh #1, then down through #2 on a slant. Simply continue as shown and, again, cut off the knot just before you reach it.

When you come to the end of the row, turn your canvas entirely around. The end of row one will become the beginning of row two and so on, and on—and on.

I don't mean this to sound like a put-down. Except for the fact that I don't approve of it as a substitute for basket weave, the continental is quite a serviceable stitch and has several virtues.

First, it's excellent used as an outline to separate areas you will later fill in with basket weave.

Second, and I think more important, it's marvelous for border work and I constantly use the stitch for this purpose. Since borders are right-angled, you will turn a corner like this—

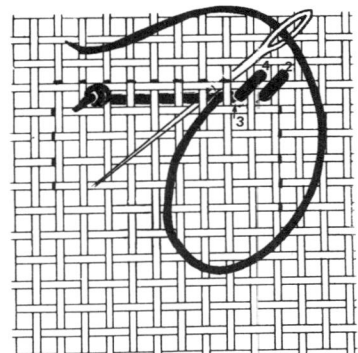 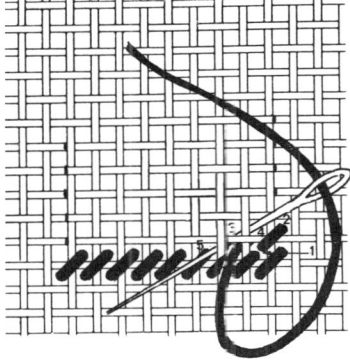 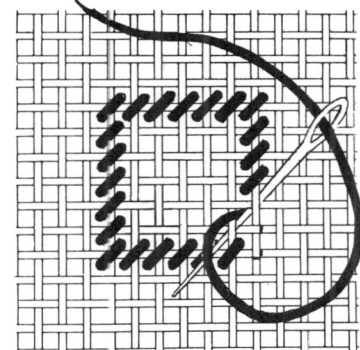

Steps in the continental stitch.

In different colors the continental stitch makes a nice border.

I do a switch with the continental, which I've a sneaky feeling may not be approved in the best needlepointing circles, but I like the effect I achieve somewhat illegitimately. Perhaps you will too.

One day I looked at the wrong side of a line of continental stitches I'd just made, and I found myself thinking what a fine, fat, dimensional effect it had—rather like Manueline rope carving. Instead of going on thinking it would be nice if it looked like that on the front, I put it there.

By turning my canvas over and, working from the back just as though the back were the front, I got exactly what I wanted. Naturally you will anchor your beginning and ending threads on the false front side.

If you do this stitch in different, or alternating colors, the look is particularly stylish.

If you try this backside-to stitch, I warn you to be most careful not to split your yarn as you work. The rope will look frayed if you do.

The brick stitch

You needn't be a bricklayer to understand why this stitch is so named. Each individual stitch is laid exactly as a brick is laid, and as logically.

This is really only a second-cousin in the large Gobelin-bargello-Florentine family but, because it's such a useful, tractable, satisfactory background stitch, let's talk about it before we approach the more formidable members of the clan.

You'll begin your first stitch on the left this time. Proceed to the right, then **go back** and come forth on alternating levels. There'll be no nonsense about turning the canvas upside down here.

ALL ABOUT STITCHES

Instead of using the knot device for starting, I find it easier to leave a short, temporary strand of yarn at the beginning of the initial row. After you've anchored your first yarn length, thread this into the needle and weave over and under the first few stitches until it's secured.

Begin the up and down line of stitches as shown.

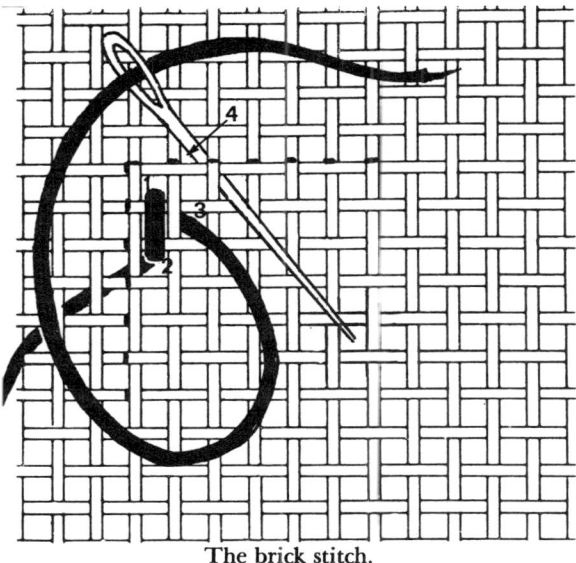

The brick stitch.

Stagger your stitches as illustrated until you've reached your boundary, then travel back from right to left in the following manner.

Insert your needle two meshes below the last stitch you made. Bring it back up through the last mesh in row one, then over one mesh so that it's two meshes below the second-to-last stitch. From this point, you won't need instruction; simply place stitch between stitch. You'll be laying your bricks downward, rather than up from bottom to top, but no matter. It's the same principle.

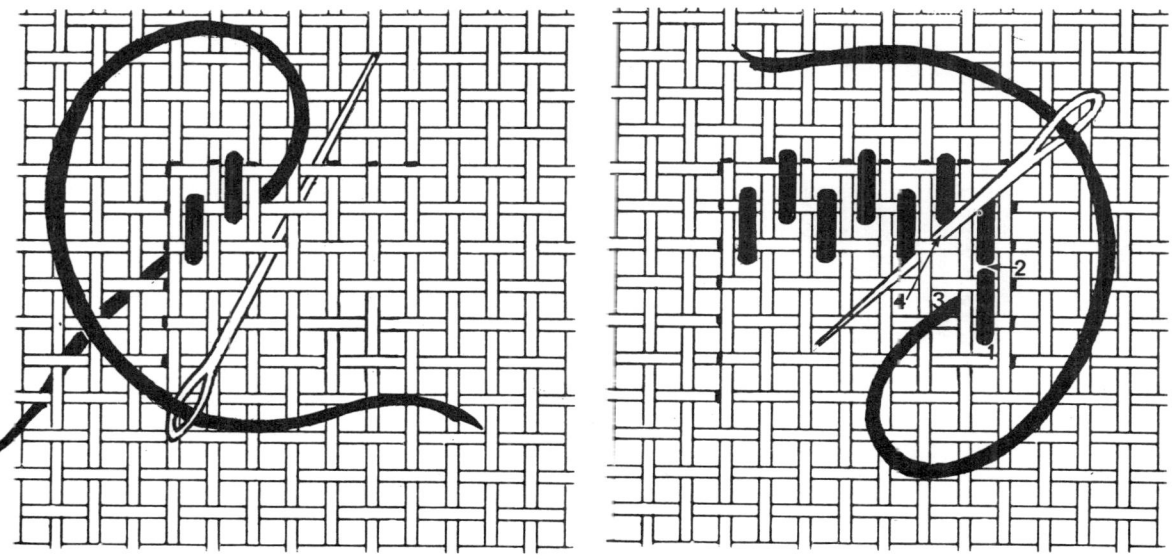

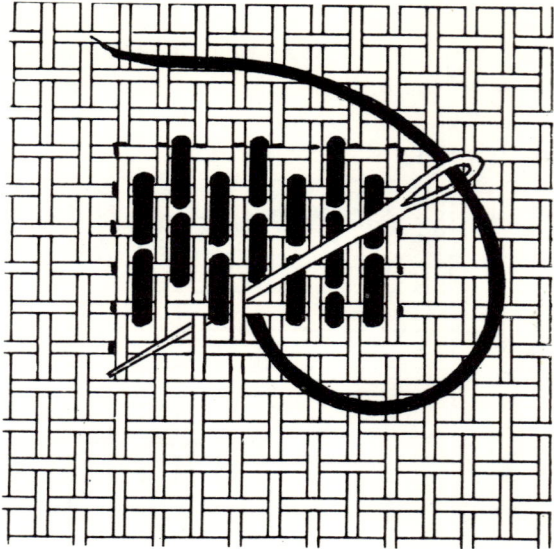

You'll use this stitch for backgrounds on mono canvas. It fills large and small areas swiftly and attractively. It's so mindlessly manageable, you can stitch away and think about four other things at the same time.

Should you be wondering what to do about those snaggle teeth at the bottom and top of the canvas, don't panic. Fill them in with half a stitch, thusly—

A finished area of the brick stitch will look like this—

When you're filling-in around a design—presumably one you've done in basket weave—you'll use this same system. Just add half a stitch wherever necessary.

The only pitfall to avoid when you do brick stitch is yarn that's too thin. It's

An area filled in with the brick stitch.

ALL ABOUT STITCHES

quite possible you'll need to add an extra ply in order to avoid exposed vertical canvas threads. If, for example, you used two plies of Persian wool for the design, make it three for the brick background.

And relax with this stitch—don't pull the yarn too tightly.

Now that you've learned the basket-weave and the brick stitches you can cover a lot of background, and these two are really the only ones you'll need for the purpose. I've experimented with others but, although the textures they produce are often very interesting, either they've been incredibly slow, or they've tortured my canvas into weird and not very wonderful shapes—or both. Although blocking will usually bring a canvas back to a reasonably normal shape, I still prefer stitches that are less assertive.

The Florentine family

This method of stitchery dates back to something like the fourteenth-century. It's been used to embroider papal vestments and has embellished the hangings for royal canopied beds. Entire books have been written about these stitches as well as their history, and museums are stuffed with examples of this ancient art.

The family tree has many branches and even more numerous twigs. You'll find these referred to, variously, as Florentine, bargello, Hungarian point, Parisian stitch, Gobelin and the brick stitch you just learned. Actually, many of these names are simply interchangeable, and any differences are subtle indeed. The most important fact to remember is that they are essentially the same. Like little elevators, they travel in two directions only—up and down.

Though direction is circumscribed, your stitches may follow historical patterns handed down from the earliest needleworkers, or they can go wildly contemporary—even psychedelic, if you like.

These vertical stitches can be worked over threads in your canvas from one, up to a possible eight. Frankly, I think a leap over even six threads isn't a very practical notion if you happen to have children, pets, parties, bracelets, buttons or even fingernails. Those long stitches aren't exactly snag-proof. A span of two to four meshes always seems sensibly practical when you're working on 14- to 10-count canvas.

The Gobelin stitch

This stitch travels along on one level to form even ridges not unlike a horizontal corduroy. Actually, all these Florentine stitches are textural in appearance and often seem more like woven cloth than conventional needlepoint tapestry.

The upright Gobelin on the next page is laid over three canvas threads (two meshes). It can be done successfully over more or fewer, but this is the number I like. As with brick stitch, you'll begin at the left and work back and forth.

This time you may anchor your thread with the usual knot, placed to the right of the starting point.

Bring the needle from back to front through one mesh, then insert it two meshes directly below. Just place upright stitches all in a row, neatly, side by side until you reach your boundary.

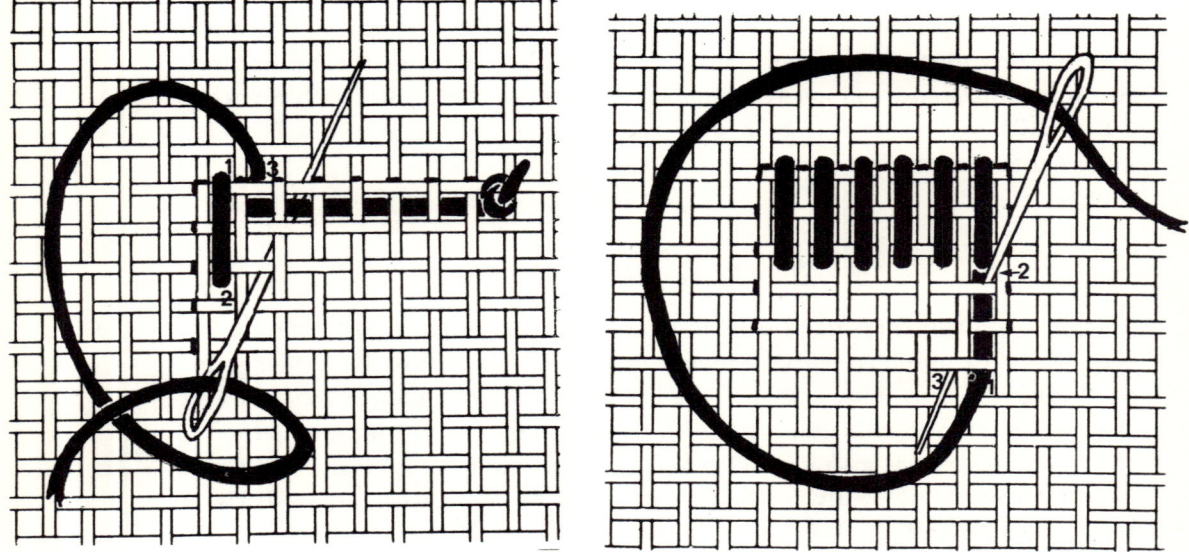

The Gobelin stitch.

To begin row two, bring the needle down two meshes directly below your last stitch in row one. Now take it up to meet the bottom of this same stitch, as shown. You will simply proceed to the right, just as you did from the left. Done properly, a few rows of the Gobelin stitch will look like this

The Gobelin stitch is a good background stitch.

ALL ABOUT STITCHES

Again, as in all stitches of this family, be sure your yarn stays plump and untwisted so it will fill the canvas properly.

Gobelin can be used as a background stitch to fill in around stitches of other types, but I think it works best in its own company exclusively.

The chair seat (Fig. 18, after p. 96) is an example of what I mean; an entire rug done in these wide-waled horizontal rows is texturally unique. It is true that the design should be planned in straight geometrics, or within the bounds of stylized forms. If you think of the beauty and variety of pattern which came off the ancient looms of Eastern weavers, you'll scarcely feel restricted.

I don't remember having seen a modern rug made in this ropy stitch before I came to Madeira, and now I long to experiment with one on my own. Although I'm not certain of this, I suspect the hand-made Gobelin rugs I've come across in a factory here may be more or less the invention of its talented director. I do know the effective contemporary designs are his alone.

Flame variations

The patterns these stitches create have been turning up in commercially woven fabrics for some years now, but the fact that those eternal flames leap endlessly over yard after yard of machine-loomed cloth makes their needlepoint possibilities no less alluring.

Except for the usual directional restrictions, there are no unbreakable rules for these particular Florentine stitches. Flame patterns may be infinitely varied; they can be plotted into traditional repeats that reach back into antiquity. On the other hand, you may be as inventive as you like and, if you really give your needle its head, you could be in for some wildly wonderful surprises.

Where color is concerned, you're permitted the same wide latitude. Combine with abandon, or restrict your choice to subtle shadings of only one hue. It all depends on what you want to say and how forcefully you want to say it.

The flame stitches, in all their myriad guises, need to be counted if precision is your goal. If you plan a complicated series of hurdles, it's a good idea to map them on graph paper first. Follow the draft with close attention until every move and jump has been established.

Before you think of attacking anything so complex, however, I suggest you begin with an elementary uphill, downhill project. You'll need to count meshes for the first row only. After that, just keep building as indicated below. Again, it's best to eliminate the knot. Leave that bit of yarn dangling until the needle is free to weave it into your initial stitches.

You may want to group stitches for more interesting textural differences, but the basic sequence will be the same.

For a brocaded effect which looks impossibly intricate (but isn't at all), graduate the length of your stitches.

If you reverse your canvas, and stand the zigs and zags on their heads, you'll come up with diamond shapes.

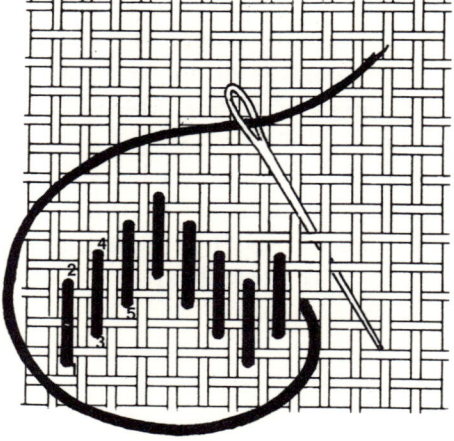

The flame stitch.

The flame stitch with the length of the stitches graduated.

Put all these suggestions together for real, and you'll have created something like this—

All this is no more than bedrock beginnings to what can become a very complex sort of stitchery. For more complete guidance and inspiration, I suggest

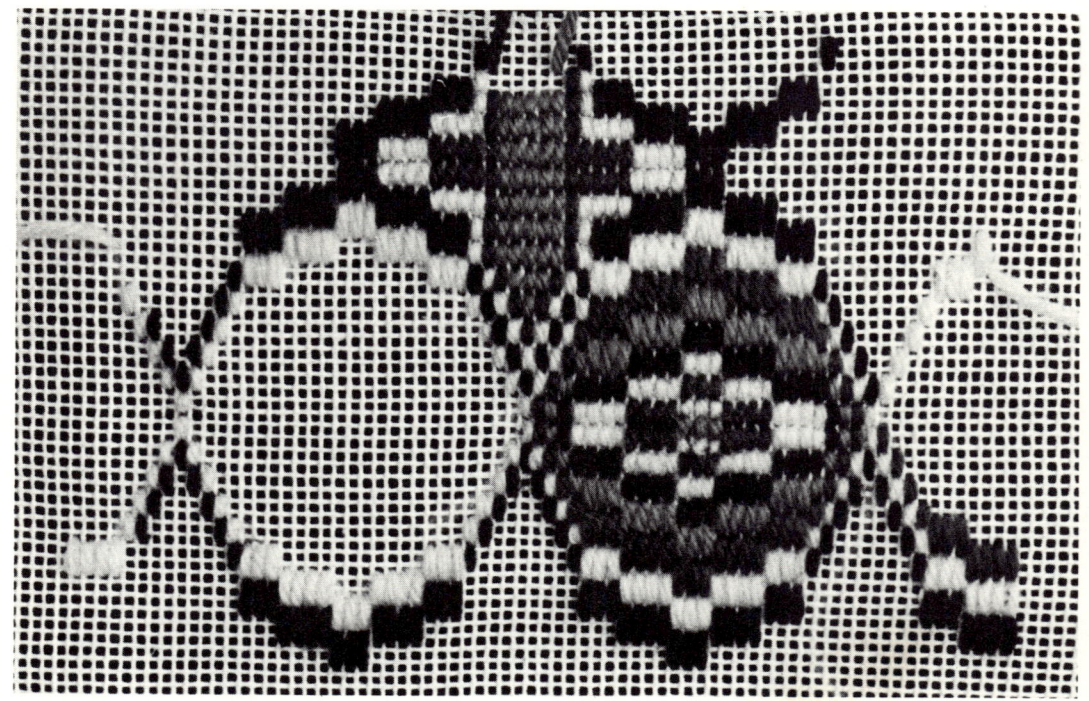

A design of flame stitches.

ALL ABOUT STITCHES

a small book called *Bargello,* by Elsa S. Williams. If you're interested in pursuing this special needlepoint form, you'll find the clear illustrations invaluable.

The herringbone stitch

This is a stitch with a sturdy, homespun look to it. It works best on canvas with a not too small mesh count. Ten is an excellent choice, which makes it ideal for backgrounding a small rug.

The stitch zips along at a fine rate when the meshes are large enough. If they aren't, it's not only painfully slow to work, the whole texture message somehow gets lost.

This time you're on one-way streets. There's no traveling back and forth from left to right to left again, and you won't turn your canvas either. When a row is finished, just secure the end of your thread and return to GO. You'll come back to the head of the line at the left and do each row separately and in turn.

Angle your stitches as shown in the diagram below—one after the other like little tepees.

Steps in the herringbone stitch.

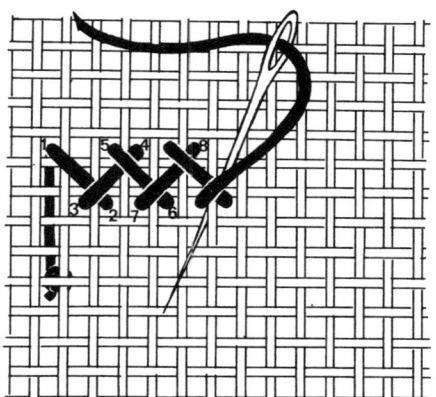 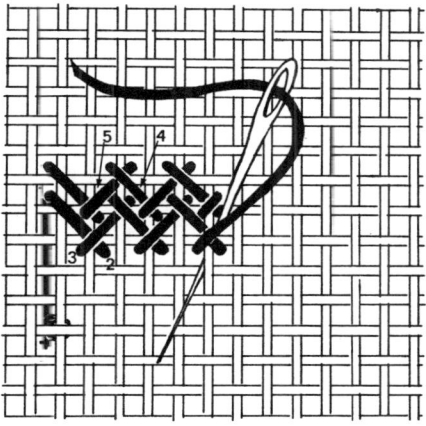

The second, and all subsequent rows will exactly duplicate the first. Start each row one mesh lower than the preceding one.

Your finished practice square will look like this, if you've worked it on 10-count canvas.

Finished rows of the herringbone stitch.

A few fancy stitches

Any of these stitches could cover an entire surface, I imagine. I just never use them that way. I like to give them special decorative assignments, which means I mostly let them go to work in borders.

The Smyrna stitch

Though this one sounds exotically oriental, really it's nothing more than a corpulent cross-stitch. It makes a lumpy, bumpy chain which looks precisely like a string of beads.

You can create extra interest by alternating the colors of your beads, by making them into double or triple strands and by edging the rows with inside-out continental stitch.

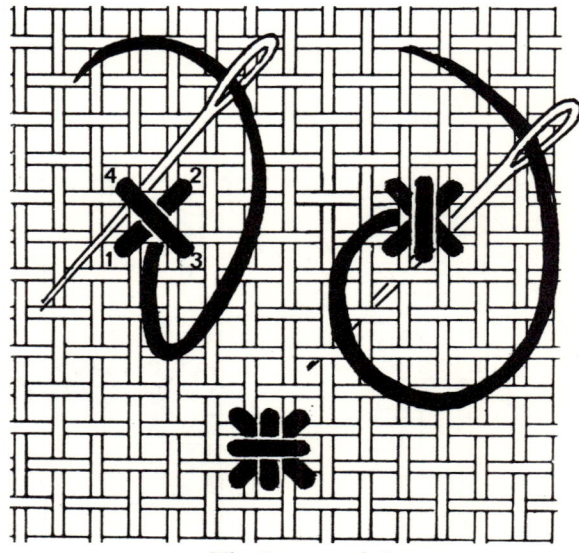

The Smyrna stitch.

This probably looks more complicated than it really is. In fact, there's nothing more to it than a superimposition of the slanting cross-stitch over the upright. This gives you a double cross and a lot of dimension.

As usual, be careful to cross over in the same direction for each stitch.

This photograph will show you one way to use the Smyrna stitch effectively.

A row of Smyrna stitches.

ALL ABOUT STITCHES 59

The Scotch stitch

Since this stitch forms a distinct check rather than anything resembling a plaid, I can't think why it's called Scotch. Let's say it's bonnie and let it go at that.

This is an adaptable stitch. You can make the threads within the squares slant in one direction, or you can pigeon-toe them into a chevron. You can make alternate squares in a second color, or a second stitch, and these latter variations will produce a true checkerboard look.

Four variations of the Scotch stitch.

You may work these square sections either horizontally or diagonally. Whichever way you go, the first square is begun in exactly the same fashion.

To proceed horizontally, start your second square in the upper left-hand corner just as you did with the first. Bring the needle up from the bottom of square one to the top of square two.

To travel diagonally, place your needle as shown below. If you're alternating with another color or with continental stitch this is the simpler procedure. For the second color or stitch, place the next diagonal row alongside the one preceding it.

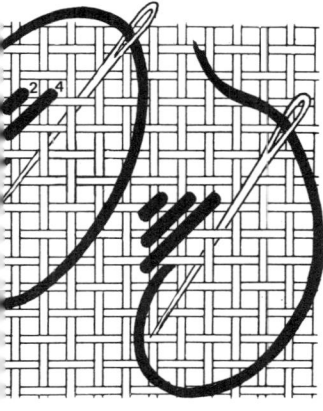 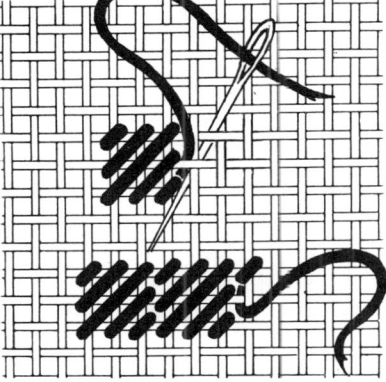 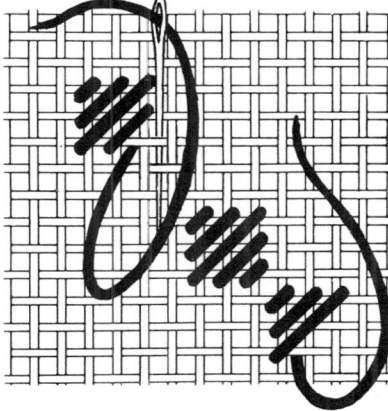

The Scotch stitch.

I especially like this Scotch stitch for borders, but I have, at times, used it for entire backgrounds. It doesn't pull the canvas out of shape and it's fairly fast to do. For most projects I find it too busy, but there are times when a complex texture is desirable.

Keep in mind that it doesn't fill in around a design very well. The best way to handle this problem is to bring the squares as close as you can to your motif, then close the gaps with a nimbus of basket weave in the background color.

The triangle stitch

This is a pretty little geometric stitch that lends itself to all manner of lively ideas.

I could never imagine working this stitch (which is really a combination of stitches) into any extensive area. Used with other, less complex types and as a sort of connecting link, it's most effective.

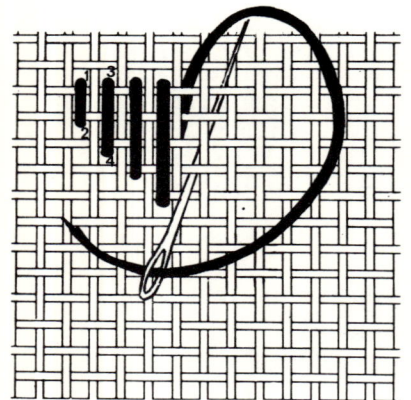 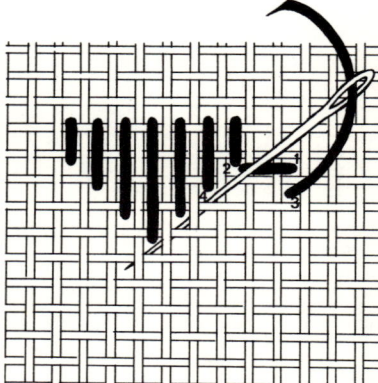 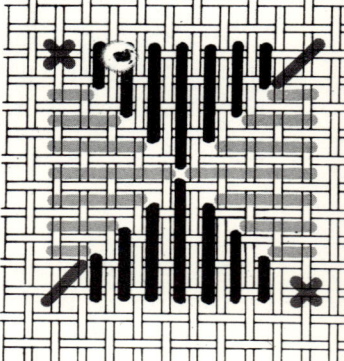

The triangle stitch.

The triangle can add much interest to borders; you can lay these little nested pyramids in a line, or space them widely or confine them to corners only.

While all components could be done in one color, I like using three—one for each set of 2 triangles and a third for the fill-in crosses at the corners of the square.

This stitch quite obviously doesn't travel with great speed, but it isn't one you'll use every day, nor will you spread it lavishly over any canvas. Keep it in mind, however, it's often useful and it's simple to do.

Borders

Paintings take on additional importance when they've been given proper frames, and a border around your needlepoint design can give you the same happy result. Anything from a large rug to the smallest pillow will quite often be improved enormously if it has an edging of some sort to contain the background and keep it from bleeding off into space.

A frame should enhance without overshadowing whatever it surrounds, and its style must be appropriate to the picture inside. A needlepoint border will abide by these same rules. Although, at times, it can become an integral part of the central motif and, therefore, have great importance, mostly it should not intrude very much. A few lines of inside-out continental stitch (page 50) are often as much as you'll need for framing. They'll be the equivalent of "strip molding" around a picture. Sometimes I add no more than a "mat" of basket-weave for delineation. More usually, this is a situation which gives you an opportunity to frolic around with slightly unusual stitches. These will accent rather than detract from the whole, especially if you use texture rather than color contrast to build your enclosure.

The really big thing to remember when you're plotting a border is the importance of knowing for certain exactly how many meshes you've allowed for your design. You can't just take off from one corner and expect to find precisely the number of stitches you need to complete the last motif waiting for you at the other end. This would constitute a miracle.

Unless you're about to stitch nothing more complicated than a series of lines around the canvas, you must plan a plot and count. Carefully divide the meshes from center to outer corners—then do it again, just to be certain. It's a terribly good idea to indicate the allotted spaces with your gray felt pen and, if you want to embark on something intricate, better map it all out on graph paper first.

In Fig. 13, after p. 64 you'll find some border ideas. Some incorporate the off-beat stitches just described; others are designs worked out with more prosaic, meat-and-potatoes stitches. These prototypes can be adapted and changed in a dozen different ways. All have possibilities for use as frames for your needlepoint projects and, if you readjust your thinking a little, wouldn't most of them make smashing belts as well?

How to make a braid trim

There are all sorts of involved methods of twisting and twining wool together to form a braid. If you really want to learn how to execute them, I suggest you invest in a handcraft book, or make friends with an old sailor. Since your trim should merely blend, rather than take over in breadth or intricacy, you should be content with an unassuming, uncomplicated plait.

To begin, it's important to have uncut skeins of wool to work with, so ask the needlework shop to leave the hanks intact. After you've used all you need for the trimming, you can cut the remainder to proper length for future needlepointing. Right now, you need longer strands—that is, unless you want to piece them together, and that's a job-and-a-half. It can be done, but it's fussy and irritating, so avoid it if possible.

Presumably you'll combine three different shades or, perhaps, three distinctly different colors but, even if you plan a one-color braid, you'll divide the wool into groups of three to be folded one over the other. The number of strands in each group (or set) will depend on how thick you want the trim to be, and on the type of wool you'll be using.

A nice flat braid, a little less than a half-inch wide is a good finish for any average chair or bench. To make this, you'll need four strands of tapestry wool for each set (twelve strands in all), or three of Persian wool (nine in all).

Before you cut lengths from the skein (or skeins if you're using three shades) be certain they'll be long enough. Use a tape measure to estimate how much trim you'll need to go around the bottom edge of the seat.

To give you an idea of yardage, the dining chairs (Fig. 7, after p. 32) require a little more than 50 uninterrupted inches of finished braid, plus another foot for the space between the two back supports, while the small bench (Fig. 9, after p. 64) measures a little more than 5 feet around. The longest span you're apt to cope with will probably be the edging for the seat of an armchair. Here you can count on at least 9 unbroken, running feet. The shorter lengths for outlining the back section and arm pieces can be braided separately.

The strands you cut will be longer, of course, than your tape measurement. A good way of determining just how much longer is to remember that approximately 1/6 of the length will be lost in the braiding process. For example, if you start out with yard-long strands, the finished trim will measure only 30 inches. Allow for this loss—and more for safety's sake. Don't scrimp!

Divide the wool strands into threes or fours, depending on the type of wool you're using. Now, join the sets with a piece of masking tape to hold them in place. Over this starting point, clamp one of those paper clips with a vice-like grip. You can buy these in any stationery shop.

Find something solid and stable on which to hook the ring at the top of your clip. The strands must be held *gently* taut as you braid. I suggest you do the job

ALL ABOUT STITCHES

A braid of three different colors, three strands to each color.

standing up so you can walk away from the mooring as the strip grows.

The process of laying one strand over another is quick and easy. Just pretend you're plaiting an exceptionally long pigtail—Rapunzel's maybe. If her braid gets too long, re-clip it somewhere closer to your position. We don't want you walking out the window. Incidentally, it's a smart idea to have a second clip handy. If you're forced to stop along the way to answer the telephone, the strands will stay neatly in place.

Keep a steady tension so the braid will be regular and even. When you come to the end, tie it securely with a bit of yarn so the plait won't begin to ravel. Finish off the beginning in the same way—it's safer than the masking tape.

Give your finished trim to the upholsterer along with your needlepoint. He'll know how to glue and invisibly tack it to whatever he's covering. Warn him not to pull it, however. You want it to lie flat and snug. If you've skimped, he'll have no choice other than to stretch the braid to fit, so give him a litttte more than you estimated.

How to make a cord

If you didn't learn how to do this slip-and-slide, chain-looped cord with a length of kitchen string when you were a child, you were underprivileged. I'm sorry about that but, cheer up, it's not too late.

Though it's possible to make this cord just by holding the length of yarn in your two hands (it's rather like crocheting without a hook), I prefer to tie one end to a drawer handle or a chair back. As you did with the braid trim, you'll walk away from the starting post as the chain lengthens.

Again, in order to make the cord long enough, you'll work with yarn from an uncut skein. Two or three strands of Persian or tapestry wool are required to give your cord heft and importance. If you can find a heavy rug wool in the color you want (you usually can, for the range is wide), use this, singly, instead. I much prefer it to multiple strands. It's easier to work with and guarantees an even chain.

In order to estimate how long a strand you'll need, first decide the length of your finished cord. Multiply this by nine, then add some extra inches for beginning and ending.

If your cord is to be used for a loose chair or bench cushion, add two additional feet to the measurement—or a foot to dangle at each corner for tying around the legs. Thus, if you have needlepointed a 16-inch square cushion, you will make four cords, each 40 inches long. Multiplied by nine, you will need strands of yarn 10 yards long (360 inches)—plus an added foot for waste. You now begin to realize why you must work from an uncut skein.

After you've secured one end of the strand to some handy object, fold the yarn as near as possible to the starting point and make a slip knot.

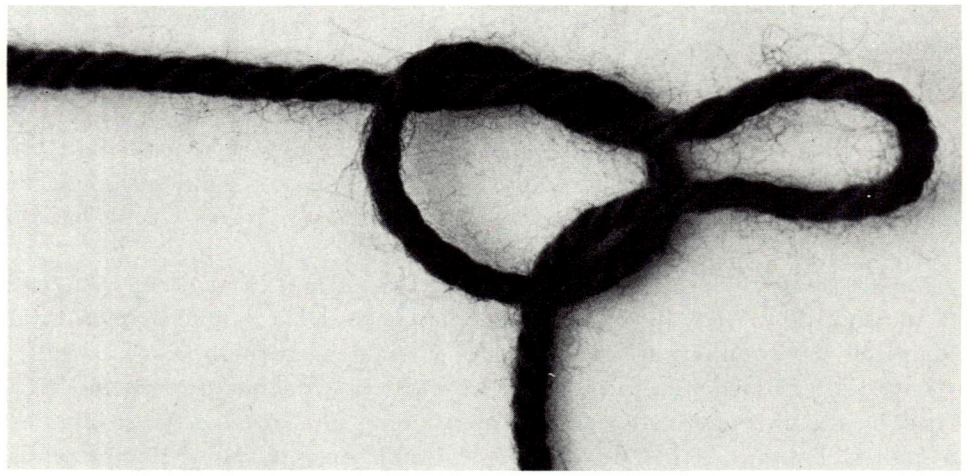

Making a cord is like crocheting without a crochet hook.

Keep drawing loop through loop to form what's nothing more nor less than a detached chain stitch. Keep the loops small, and draw each through the other with even tension so every link is identical.

This is true idiot's delight and you can whip out a long chain in a matter of minutes but, in spite of that, you'll have made a very good-looking cord—a strong one too.

The way to end the chain when you've reached the limit of your yarn length is to pull the last loop all the way through until it no longer *is* a loop. If you

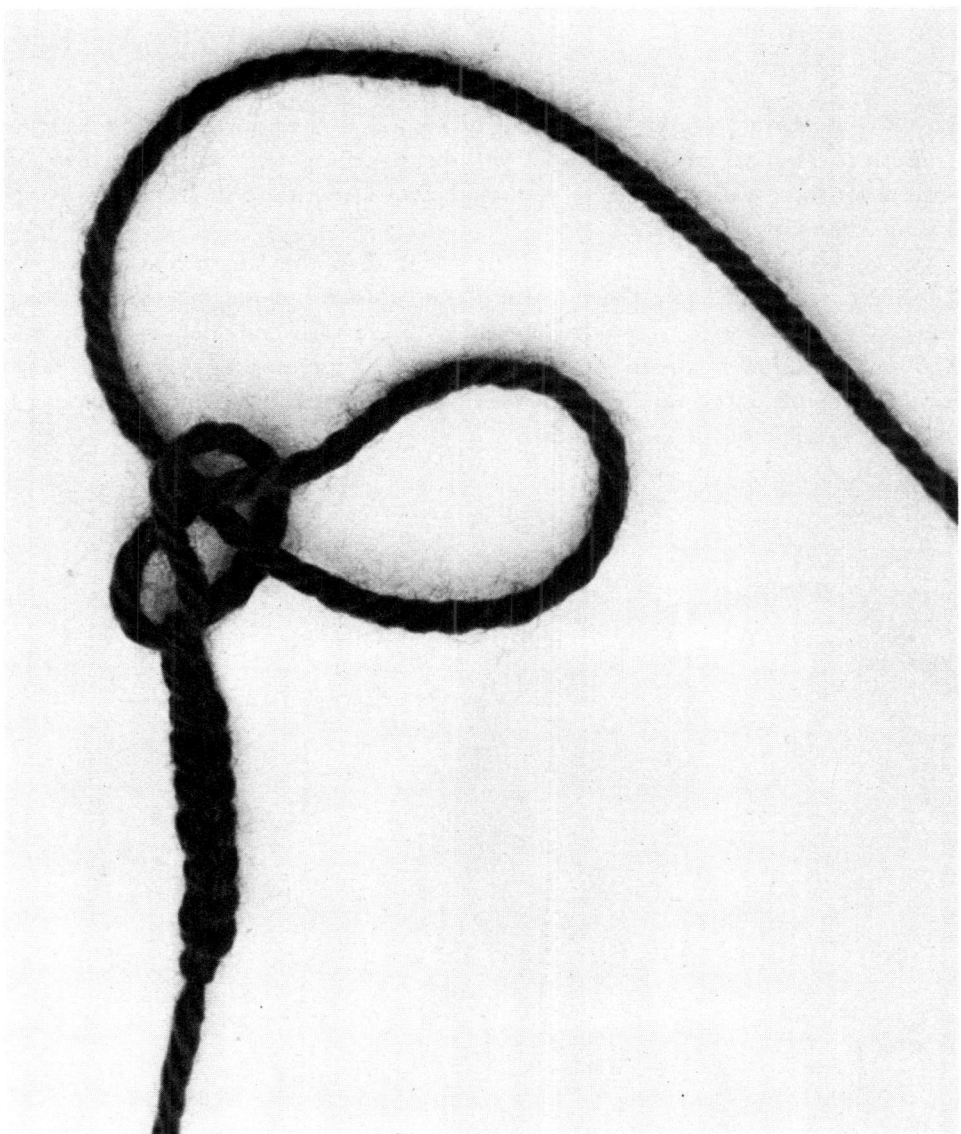

don't do this, the whole chain is apt to disappear like an ice cube on a hot stove.

Doubtless you'll want to attach a tassel to the cord ends, so don't pull the thread too tightly when you lock the last link. Leave it just loose enough to be pulled out and later replaced. See tassels in the section to follow.

Just in case you don't want a tassel for some reason, then do pull the lock stitch tightly. Thread the loose end into a needle and weave it neatly through a few of the chains.

The cord can be blind-stitched to the edge of your cushion. Sew it from the underside with wool of the same color.

How to make a tassel

If you've used rug wool for your cord, it's a good idea to make the tassel of the same yarn. Tapestry or Persian wool will do the job as well, but you'll need to wind a lot more yarn. The more you wind, the fatter, more important and professional the tassel will look.

Cut a piece of cardboard just a little wider than the length you want your finished tassel to be. Wrap the yarn round and round, but not too tightly. When you feel there's enough, stop winding and snip the yarn end. Between forty and fifty times around is about right for a tassel 3½ inches long. A longer tassel seems to require more wool. When you've reached your limit, tie a short length of yarn through the loops as shown.

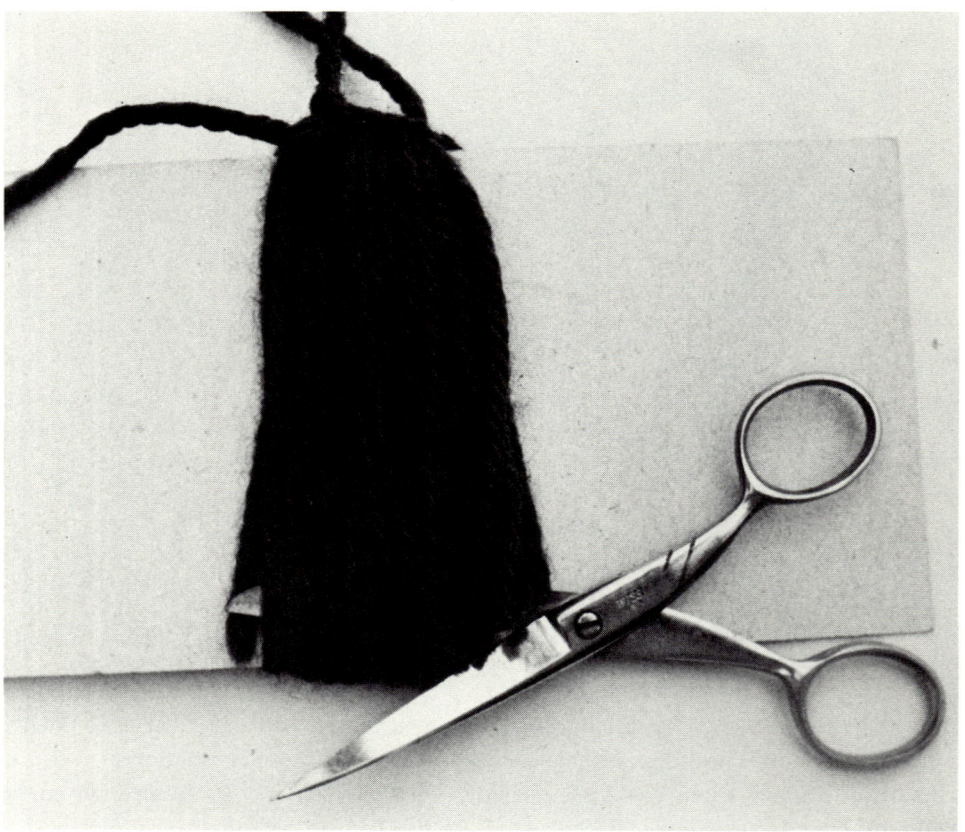

Steps in making a tassel.

Slip your scissors through the loops at the bottom and cut carefully. You want all the strands to be equal. If you're planning to attach the tassel to the end of a cord, turn the whole bunch upside down, so the knot you just made is on the

ALL ABOUT STITCHES 67

underside and cut those ends to match the others. If the tassels are to be used as trim for the four corners of a pillow, leave the knot and ends on top. See pillow mounting, page 102.

To join cord to tassel, take your length of chain stitch and unlock the last stitch (pull the last link out a little). Force the end of the yarn under the loop at the top of the tassel, then replace it through the chain link as shown. Pull tightly to lock, and cut the yarn end so it becomes part of the tassel.

To attach a tassel to the other end or the cord (the beginning), loosen the first stitch and repeat the procedure described above. The only difference will be that the first link won't pull out as the last one does.

Smooth the bundle of yarn so all the strands fall straight. Cut a short strand of yarn (7 or 8 inches long) and wrap it a number of times around the tassel about 3/4 of an inch from the top. If you've used rug wool, divide the strand in half, otherwise it will be too bulky. Tie the two ends firmly, then thread them into a needle. Conceal them in the head of the tassel.

Give the whole thing a good shake and trim off any uneven strands at the bottom. You'll have as professional a tassel and cord as ever came out of a designer's showroom.

FIGURE 9 The author's first needlepoint project. Notice the braid trim.

FIGURE 10 A chair seat of the Gobelin stitch incorporating the crossed center line into the design.

FIGURE 11 Woven ribbon design.

FIGURE 12 Beserk bargello flame stitch —wild, free flowing and colorful.

FIGURE 13 Examples of border ideas.

FIGURE 14 Colors that seem companionable when looked at separately, but neutralize each other when stitched side-by-side.

FIGURE 15 The same colors as in group I, but recombined with either white or another color to bring each tint out separately.

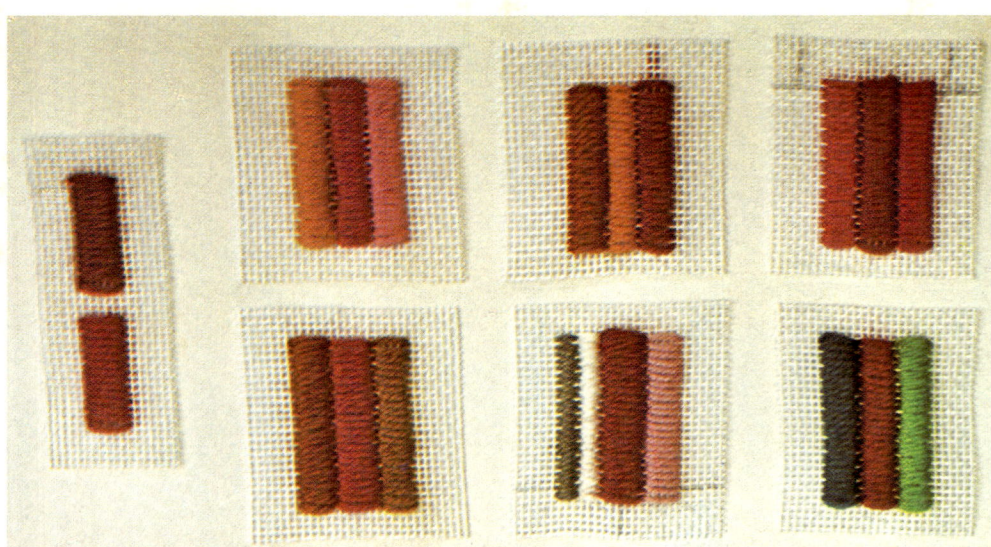

FIGURE 16 The two reds are at the same intensity but notice how their color "seems" to change when stitched next to these other colors.

IV

Color

Your design is complete and beautifully drawn on canvas—or on paper—or is just in your head, depending on what type of needlepoint stitch and method you've chosen to execute.

If you've adapted something totally, you need only duplicate the original as closely as possible. Should you wish to make changes; if the model you used was black and white, or if this is your own creation, you must now think about color and what you want it to say.

Individual reactions to color vary immensely. They can range from mild pleasure to fierce joy in some people, but a too large majority will run scared for the safe cover of neutrals. Having known a good many of these latter unfortunates as clients, I've concluded they believe color selection requires a working knowledge of witchy charms and appropriate incantations. There's magic in color, of course, but it has nothing very much to do with the old black variety.

How to choose colors

Don't be afraid of color. With a little understanding and intelligent handling, it's a very tractable animal, but you must recognize its moods and know, for instance, that it can be alternately prudent, extravagant, artless or worldly depending entirely on how you use it. It can stand right up, or just lie around not doing very much of anything. Shades of the same hue will range from warm, to hot, to burning while, at the other end of the spectrum-thermometer, there are the cold, bleak tones as opposed to those equally cold, but invigorating. Make yourself aware that cool may mean tender-as-spring, or tepid as hour-old bath water.

Colors that can turn one person on, may switch another right off, and you should find out which does what for you. Look around the rooms you live in. Flip through your clothes closet and the drawer where you keep your scarves. You'll find there's a kind of story here, and it repeats itself more often than you would have suspected. Heed it. It's important to select colors you like, and like to have around you. Learning how to combine these in a piece of needlepoint is another thing.

Poke among the yarn bins at a needlework shop if you can. Shuffle paint sample chips if you can't. When you stop and say, "That's really a very swell color!" the chances are good that, for you, it *is* really a very swell color. Mix it with several others you like and see what can happen. Unexpectedly, the most vibrant shade will sometimes neutralize itself into oblivion when it's teamed with another of equal intensity. Try separating these, or eliminate one and introduce a substitute. Quite often the tame cat turns savage; the once dull tonal values become brilliant chroma, gaudy as carnivals. In the same fashion, you may wish to lower the key and play it all very piano. By juxtaposing the identical tints and hues in different positions and mixtures you'll come up with an astonishing variety of inspired palettes, and with some very uninspired ones thrown in too.

Not only can colors be made to appear tranquil or nervous; flat or flashy according to the manner in which they're combined, they will also manage to look deeper or lighter than they actually are.

Some examples of color chemistry are illustrated on page xx, but make your own experiments. Explore! Familiarize yourself with the funny things that happen when two colors meet and mate.

A few things you may not know about wool colors

WHITE WILL ALWAYS DEEPEN SURROUNDING COLORS   At the same time, it accentuates their brilliance. Thus, the addition of white in small areas will serve as a sort of reverse accent, illuminating whatever it touches. Used as a background, it can turn colors to glittering jewels.

AVOID BLACK   It's difficult to work with black yarn because, for some reason, the dye does something rather horrid to the texture of the wool. Substitute the very deepest, almost-black browns, greens, or really midnight blues. The effect will be very close to black but, as bonus, it will be richer and far less mournful, especially used as a background.

WATCH OUT FOR YELLOW   It may look whammy in the light of day. By night it can vanish in a very sneaky way. Be discriminating about what you team it with if you want it to stick around. The point is that the most vivid shade of yellow is relatively pallid compared to normal tones of most other colors.

COLOR

ALWAYS LOOK AT YOUR WOOL COLORS IN TWO LIGHTS The absolutely gorgeous color you saw at the sunny window can turn treacherous by lamplight and bleach out to insipidity. Since you probably want your needlepoint to shine by night as well as by day, you may be forced to compromise. Study the color changes effected under both lighting conditions and be guided.

Wool has a tendency to absorb light because of the depth of its texture. Sewing thread works up lighter than it appears on the spool. The opposite is true of woolen yarn. Choose a slightly paler tone than the one that looks perfect in the hank.

TONAL VALUES Be very certain these aren't too close. Two colors can be distinctly different but, worked side by side, they often wash together like wet water colors. You'll find a new-leaf green stitched next to sky blue or acid yellow will give you no contrast at all, and your design definition will be non-existent.

The junction of two grayed tones may be even more negative. My problem with Fly (Fig. 4, after p. 32) is an example of what can happen to an ill-met pair of colors. In their skeins, the beige tone I chose for the legs, and the blue of the background seemed totally unrelated. It wasn't until I'd filled in around two of the extremities I realized, from three feet distant, I'd divested the hapless fly of legs and antennae. I took the easier path in repairing this goof. Instead of picking out, I overstitched the fugitive legs with a much lighter shade than I'd used originally.

Though this was not an irreclaimable calamity, the reparation was tiresome and it did teach me to be more cautious and alert to the fact that it's all too easy for color values to merge and lose all meaning.

Put your yarns together, side by side, and look at them from a distance before you begin to stitch—not after.

BE STERN WITH ACCENT COLORS Whether they're used in music, language, painting or needlepoint, remember that accents are stresses. Their very purpose is to emphasize. If you want your highlight or shadow to be easily understood, be certain you've chosen a tone that's highly enough keyed or deep enough to make a definite point.

The company your colors keep

The rough color notes on page 70 will give you only the sketchiest sort of picture of what happens to tone and value when certain colors and shades are combined. Condensed as the story must be, the essential plot should be clear.

GROUP I (Fig. 14, after p. 64) illustrates how colors neutralize and become negative when their companions are either unsuitable, or too closely related.

Such an effect is, of course, desirable if subtle shading is what you're after but, if it's contrast you want, be certain that's what you're getting. The variation may seem sufficiently pronounced when you look at the wool separately in the skein—stitched conjunctively on canvas, the colors often lose their voices and don't speak up at all.

Half-close your eyes and look at the combinations in Group I. Each little section will become one amorphous blob without definition or interest.

GROUP II   (Fig. 15, after p. 64) shows a few of the personality changes you can achieve. In most of the examples, these are the identical colors you see combined in Group I. Separated and teamed with white or other colors, they stand up and make statements instead of sneaking off into oblivion.

This group will also illustrate the chameleon-like qualities of a few colors. Look at the middle color in combination 2, Group I. Now, compare it to the second combination in Group II. The true dark green you see in the first turns itself into an umistakable deep navy blue in the second.

The beige tone in the first figure of Group II isn't really beige at all. It's the soft yellow you see in figure 3 of the same group, and figure 3 in Group I.

Sometimes these tricky disguises will work to your advantage—more often than not, they won't. So if you're experimenting, test first by studying color reactions before you put in too many stitches.

GROUP III   (Fig. 16, after p. 64) is the story of two shades of red, each with the same value, each equally intense. Red A is the color of a garden-ripe tomato, while Red B could be stitched into a fine watermelon. They're both excellent shades and I like working with them. Sometimes one answers my purposes; sometimes the other.

Juxtaposed, they don't have much natural affinity but, used in separated areas of the same project, they're most effective. Red A, when combined with orange tones, changes to a dull brick. On the other hand, Red B loves to be with oranges. Red A is happy with brownish tones, while B finds most of them incompatible. Both become vibrant when they meet pink—though not the same pink. Like many other colors, these two are versatile, but not always predictable in their likes and dislikes.

Red A is the background for the bird's nest pillow (Fig. 4, after p. 32). It also serves as the base for the animal tapestry (Fig. 5, after p. 32). Even though the pillow and the hanging live in the same room, I would be amazed should anyone pick up the fact that the two are identical.

Red B glows in the faces of the animals in the tapestry but, placed next to the henna shade in the body of the dragon, it loses its brilliance entirely.

And so it goes, almost endlessly. When you play games with the spectrum you can expect surprises, and you'll see my earlier analogy to mixing wools like paints is quite valid.

V

Living with Needlepoint

Whether home is a one-room apartment or something considerably more grand, a little needlepoint (and often quite a lot) can go a long way toward adding warmth as well as personal involvement in its truest sense. Your contributions can be strikingly important, or you can confine them to an exquisite detail or two.

Unless you're planning to execute an exceptionally large rug, almost any piece of needlepoint will become an accent. Like a painting, it need not "match" anything in particular, but you don't want it to seem lonely and alien, either. As long as you're creating to your own custom order, your stitches may as well have a related point of view.

Resolve to avoid haphazard hodgepodge by tying your inventions—if only vaguely—each to the other as well as to their surroundings. Don't begin a project off the top of your head with some aimless notion of finding a place to put it after it's finished. Make your plan *before* you put design or needle to canvas.

If the room you have in mind (and in your house) is high-powered contemporary and you've been moved to embark on a bunch of fragile violets, you'd better do some serious rethinking. Though you might, for instance, stitch a monkey for a city-sophisticated apartment, you'd very, very rarely do a cow and, should the colors in a room be predominantly clear, clean pastels, you're not going to introduce muted brown and ochers. The idea of the eclectic blend has been around for some time now, and nearly everyone is aware that ingredients and proportions must be expertly chosen and cautiously mixed if the decorating recipe is going to work. You may choose to repeat a color or a theme. You can also take a stand on both counts. You may be as off-beat as you like, but even a single pillow should somehow relate to something else in the room for which it's intended. Since your labors will inevitably multiply, let the progeny be a friendly family group.

Ideas and inspirations

Years ago, and long before I suspected I'd be a helpless victim to wool and canvas myself, I made a carefully scaled drawing of a bit of Imari pattern for a client. One of the good needlework shops transferred the outline and helped her select the appropriate red, deep blue and gold tones. The happy result upholsters a pair of tiny footstools which still serve as an effective link to a fine collection of old Derby.

But for the fact that the client owned the charming little stools, this same idea would have been equally successful had we collaborated on a hearth rug, the seats for a pair of Sheraton chairs or, simply, a few pillows, each with a different motif lifted from the porcelain.

Collections of this sort are excellent themes for decorating. If you own such treasures, they're undoubtedly on display, so why not capitalize on them and increase the effect? Pinch parts of the designs and reproduce them on dining chair seats. If you can, make each seat different and adapt a variation of the pattern for window cornices to give the story an even stronger punch.

Whatever you've amassed—pottery, porcelain, frogs, owls, lions or Navajo baskets—your assemblage can launch you into a needlepoint theme. Should you be fortunate enough to own some Clichy glass paperweights, think how effective it would be to repeat the *mille fleurs* on canvas and, if your life is a real garden where real *fleurs* grow, you have it made for subject matter. Perhaps you're a bird watcher, or hung up on zebras, or snails—the list is endless as it is personal.

However, let's assume you're starting from scratch and have nothing other than a few oddly assorted wedding presents to show off, or maybe your rooms are unrelieved vanilla. In either case, you've got nothing going either for or against you. Here, you can compose your own score and you have a great opportunity to let your needlepoint really work for you. You might select a particular subject and let it repeat itself. Try a co-ordinated group of variations for both harmony and clout. You can achieve this with a group of hard-edge linear compositions, or choose a flower—something nice and massy like a poppy, an anemone or maybe geraniums. Stitch a whopping big, much larger-than-life blossom first, then scale it down into other versions. Gather several smaller flowers together and tie them with a ribbon bow, if you like. Scatter them over the background, and end the series with a really grand bouquet. The theme needn't be confined to pillows; put it on a couple of chair seats or the piano bench too. You can carry out the same thought with butterflies, large, small and intermediate; or any other creature you may fancy. If you find the flower studies are your pleasure, try to keep a bowl or two of the real thing around when you can. The tie-in will be more difficult if your choice has been butterflies.

Right now, I find myself faced with the bare, basic bones of a guest room which is being done over from—well, from empty. It's bright white and clear, sunny yellow. Though it's pretty and cheerful, it does lack personality, so I shall begin to needlepoint a few small pillows. At the moment, my idea is to design each with a different sun motif. This is an age-old symbol, and there are many versions to be adapted effectively. The room is yellow and so, as a general rule, is the sun. Madeira is known as *a ilha do sol,* so the whole notion seems to make pretty good sense. I know, too, from past experience, that I'll begin to find sun faces on all sorts of decorative things, from modern ash trays to curious bits which will turn up in antique shops. Before I'm quite aware, my made-up theme will have become the seed of a collection instead of the other way round.

Largely, these clean slates and cleared stages are the exception. Most of us possess something solidly fixed in our backgrounds which must be considered when anything new is added. A handsome patterned rug is the classic example, but brand new chintz at the windows rates the same respect. These will be your monitors, especially where color is involved. Remember always that you're creating an accent. Let the smallest, brightest spot in the pattern of rug or fabric serve as the largest area in your needlepoint.

Conversely, if the printed linen on the sofa is no longer young and gay, don't use it as inspiration. If you loathe the shabby, never-very-classy oriental in the living room, and your dearest wish is to discard it at the first whiff of a windfall, it's better to pretend it isn't there. They will go, but your needlepoint will stay, so let something else influence you.

Whether your surroundings are plain or fancy, stark or cluttered with boundless inspirations, think first. Stitch later. Project the idea for a needlepoint venture on your mental screen and look at it carefully. If it seems alien to your existing decorating scheme, do something else; or, if you can't let go, turn the original notion into a gift for the friend who does have the appropriate surroundings.

There's one further point to think of when you choose your project. Try not to be too discreetly polite and hushed, even if your needlepoint is going to live in the subtlest and palest of rooms. Your purpose may not be to produce anything really rowdy, still you certainly don't want all that work to sit in a corner and mumble to itself, either.

You'll find enough ideas listed below to keep you busy for some time. Make a few of them. Live with them—and enjoy them.

Projects

PILLOWS   The popular and useful pillow will in all probability be your first needlepoint endeavor, and you won't stop at one. Pillows are eye catchers, and each should be a little work of art. In addition to their decorative contribution, they're useful and very comfortable to have around. They can be made in all sizes, from mammoth ones for floor sitting to very tiny ones to fit into the back of a small chair. If you have a sewing machine, this is a project you can make, mount and finish with no outside, professional assistance. See page 102 for instructions.

CHAIRS AND BENCHES As a rule, you'll confine your needlepoint to seats alone. There are three distinct types of seat coverings and, for each, you will make a careful muslin pattern. See page 104.

SLIP SEATS are so named because that's precisely what they do. They slip in or out of the seat frame, and are constructed to fit snugly and exactly without having to be nailed in place. You'll find them used for dining chairs more often than for any other type of seating. These are very simple to cover by yourself.

LOOSE CUSHIONS are generally take-it-or-leave-it affairs. They're used for rush-bottomed or cane-seated chairs or benches to make them more attractive as well as more comfortable to sit upon. The cushions are quite separate, and aren't attached at all except by means of cords and decorative tassels tied to the legs.

The height of chair from floor to seat will determine the thickness of your cushion. If the seat is already 18 inches from the floor (the standard height for a dining chair) you will make the thinnest pad possible. Your feet will dangle if you make a boxed cushion several inches thick. Pads are quite simple to make, but I'd turn the boxed versions over to the upholsterer.

TIGHT SEATS In the "trade" this rather unattractive term simply means that the fabric covering is drawn tightly over a spring and hair construction. Clearly this is an upholstery job, and best left to the professional.

ENTIRE CHAIRS I strongly advise you to confine this venture to the *fauteuil* type of small armchair for which you will needlepoint seat, armrests and wood-framed back—inside only. The outside back is traditionally covered in a contrasting fabric. If you have any grandiose notion of taking a crack at an oversized wing chair, I'd give it up right away. Again, you will please allow the upholsterer to do his upholstering thing.

Should you already have an excess of pattern in your room, you might do this chair in a bargello repeat. The colors will blend with others around it, but it will conflict with nothing. Your covering will look like the lushest, most expensive fabric imaginable—and so it would be, if you hadn't made it yourself.

You may want to make a braid trim for this and for the tight seat chair. It's frequently difficult to find a commercial gimp that looks well with your stitches. See page 62 for instructions.

RUGS may be made in many sizes. They can be very useful, or they can just lie down and look pretty.

LIVING WITH NEEDLEPOINT

Make a hearth rug, if you have a hearth. If you haven't, make one anyway and use it beside your bed or in front of the sofa. If you put a small table on it, be sure it's lightly built without heavy legs or wide aprons. Better still, try one with a glass top. Even better than either of these suggestions, use a table made in clear lucite.

To be sure, a rug can cover a large area and very nearly fill an average room, but few among us have either enough strength or years ahead to attack anything larger say, than a 5 by 7 or, at the most, a 6 by 8. Since we're all busy doing a great many other things, it's best to stick to something we'll live long enough to enjoy using. Even a young-married is quite likely to be baby sitting for her grandchildren before a 9 by 12 is on the floor.

A 3 by 5 is a useful, decorative and manageable size. So is a narrow strip for a hall, or for the stairs—unless yours is a stately home. Anything larger must be done in sections and joined together when they're all complete. This piecing isn's awfully easy to do and, as for the blocking and mounting, they're impossible for the amateur. The finishing of rugs is best left to someone who knows exactly what he's about, but you'll find some basic instructions on page 107.

HEADBOARDS   A bed with a headboard (or head and foot boards, if that's its style) made to be upholstered, is a natural for needlepointing. These can be thoroughly masculine or ladylike as a watercress sandwich, depending on the design you choose. Use a plain, rather heavy fabric in your background color for the spread. You might needlepoint a bolster or two and/or a few pillows to match. This is another job you won't attempt yourself.

CORNICES   In the body of this chapter, I mentioned that needlepointed cornices might team up with dining chair seats. For a bedroom, they'd mate nicely with headboards too.

For this project, you'll require the co-operation of your nearby cabinetmaker or a clever carpenter. Though you quite possibly can do your own mounting, you may need to call in the draper for installation.

Have your cornice boxes made before you begin stitching so you'll be certain your measurements jibe. Plywood is the best material, and see to it that they're smoothly finished with no rough, splintery edges and corners.

It's best to stick to fairly straight lines. Fancifully scrolled valances could get you into all sorts of trouble and, besides, your design should carry the kick. See page 107 for suggestions.

TABLES   Call in the friendly cabinetmaker again and have him make a wooden cube or rectangle—very smooth, very exact. Usually, you will choose a size suitable for a small coffee table, or one to place beside a chair. If you're really ambitious, there's no reason why the same idea wouldn't be effective made tall enough to hold a lamp.

This project is wide-open for imaginative ideas. You can border each section—or not. You can make each side different, or needlepoint them two by two; always with the top in still another version of the design. As a suggestion, stitch a different shell on each of the four sides, then pile four together in a well-arranged group for the top.

A 14-inch cube is about the minimum size to consider for a little table, and you can scale this up to your preference and needs.

After you have your wooden base, this is a job you can do yourself—with care. See page 110.

Instead of slip-covering a whole block, you can needlepoint only the top of a table or cabinet with simple lines. Do this in *faux* marble, perhaps, or go capricious with *trompe l'oeil* objects arranged on the surface. Have a piece of plywood cut slightly smaller than the top of the table on which you plan to use it. You must take into account the thickness of your needlepoint. You'll have no trouble mounting this one. See page III.

Maggie Lane in her *Needlepoint by Design* has developed plan, pattern and technique for covering a whole Parsons table in needlepoint. Her directions cannot be improved upon.

If you make any of the above, I implore you to have a glass top cut to fit. The thought of a cigarette inexorably eating its way through your stitches is horrifying beyond all imagining, but spilled coffee or an overturned brandy can be as irrevocable.

WALL HANGINGS Since these do hang on the wall, they count as paintings, and they're up there to be seen. Design them thoughtfully and well if you want to look at them with pleasure.

Though you can frame your needlepoint (if size and subject ask for this treatment), I prefer the panel to be large enough and strong enough to be hung as a tapestry. The day of the sampler has long since passed us by.

Again, you can easily manage the mounting yourself, and I suggest you make the backing removable so that the piece can be washed and re-blocked when the time comes—and it will. See page 112 for instructions.

SCREENS I consider this idea very nearly as ambitious as a good-sized rug. Possibly more. However, if you have a lot of time and the perfect place for a paneled screen, by all means begin work. You'll turn the end result over to an expert craftsman, however.

FRAMES Small, delicate petit-point frames were much in vogue during past centuries, so the idea isn't brand-new; but what I have in mind is somewhat less precious.

I'm working up to something rather formidable. I have in mind a large frame for my dining room, which is pleading for an impressive mirror. Since distinctive old frames seem impossible to come by here, I shall reproduce one in needlepoint. It will be elaborate, and I may even add some bold, fool-the-eye carving. Any good border design will also adapt itself to this treatment but, whatever you choose, be very accurate with your measurements because you will miter your corners, and the joinings must be smooth and exact.

Incidentally, this framing idea lends itself better to a mirror than to anything pictorial.

Though that cabinetmaker (who is now quite accustomed to your kinky notions) may be able to cope with the basic structure, it might be better to go to a frame maker with your problem. A frame involves a simple but specific construction. To be technical, it must be rabbeted. If you aren't familiar with this term, a rabbet is simply a deep notch into which something can be fitted—like a door inside its frame. A framer understands this very well, while a carpenter may not.

Unfinished wood frames can sometimes be purchased in art supply stores, but be certain you choose one wide enough. It should measure from 2½ inches to 4 or even 5, depending on the expanse of mirror you want to use.

Although you can piece together and mount the needlepoint yourself, leave the mirror-fitting and installation to a professional.

* * *

A few small items which appear to be accepted handiworked additions to the home decor haven't been included in my list. Firescreens are, I feel, as much of an affectation as the ubiquitous bellpull. Neither serves any functional purpose—especially the bellpull. If it were attached to a bell, for whom would it toll these days?

I'm not much for needlepoint-covered bricks to be used as doorstops, either. For me, they're toe-breakers. Besides, since I have twenty-one interior doors in my island house which can (and often do) blow shut, the idea is a little overwhelming.

I couldn't bring myself to cover a scrap basket in needlepoint because, no matter how beautifully and originally executed, they manage to look as though they came out of some fancy closet shop.

However, these are purely personal hang-ups. You may want to stitch them all and, aside from that bellpull, I have no objection.

Any of the suggestions I've listed can adapt themselves admirably to nearly any room, but beware of floor, to up-the-wall, to ceiling stitches. If you're compulsive as well as nimble-fingered, you may find your house is beginning to look a little like the display in a large needlework shop. A needlepoint table, sitting on a needlepoint rug in front of a sofa piled high with dozens of needlepoint pillows isn't exactly the idea.

Should you see this coming, start a project that'll take you several years to complete, and break the monotony with gifts and a few things with which to decorate yourself instead of your interiors.

VI

The Stand-ins

The conventional and, I daresay, the logical course to follow in the creation of any piece of needlepoint is to begin at the beginning and continue doggedly from design conception to the last anchored stitch of background or border. After the finished project has been blocked and, perhaps, even mounted, another can move into place and be blessed with a like degree of loyalty and devotion.

This perfectly rational manner of working is great for anyone who simply likes to have a bit of take-it-or-leave-it fancy work at hand but, when you needlepoint a lot; for pleasure, for relaxation and/or the fulfillment of big creative urges—bluntly, if you're hooked—you'll appreciate and profit by this system of plural production. (If you're embarked on your first few needlepoint ventures, it's a little early for this sort of juggling. File for future use.)

A collection of partly finished scraps of needlepoint, each begun with burning eagerness; each put aside out of apathy or boredom, is a scatterbrained waste, and not what I have in mind at all. Two (or maybe more) honestly planned enterprises is something else again. Painters often work on several canvases concurrently, and so can you.

Like those of the painter, your subjects will be in various stages of development. You'll approach them at different times, in different situations and for different reasons.

I'll cite one or two basic motives to prove how sound it is to have dual or triple needlepoint projects in work simultaneously. Though you will doubtless invent your special formula, some of my own stratagems should prove helpful. Just remember that planning and discipline are requisite.

Let's assume you've found happiness with some very ambitious, monstrous big canvas which is obviously going to take an infinity to complete. Although

you're utterly devoted, there are times when even the most solid union should be temporarily sundered and only good will come of it.

Plainly, such a bundle of stitches can't go out to dinner with you, and it very likely shouldn't go away for a weekend, either. Besides it being physically impossible to fling this expanse about with anything approaching grace and airy nonchalance, the very bulk of your work bag is unconditionally guaranteed to alarm the most unflapable hostess.

Even if the piece never leaves home, it may be difficult for your own guests to feel wanted when they find you cozily tucked up under something the size of a steamer rug.

An amplitude of wool and canvas like this can't very well slip into your handbag for a trip to the hairdresser. It's no good if you're convalescing and aren't in fighting shape. Obviously it isn't the thing to pick up casually while you wait for late dinner guests, and it's surely not the needlepoint to take traveling. But that's a section all to itself.

Your involvement may, of course, be an undertaking which, though normal in size, requires perfect lighting and a really intense degree of concentration. Under any of the previously mentioned circumstances, albeit for diverse reasons, you'll find this canvas as difficult to handle as the giant project.

Since allowing those clever fingers to languish idly in your lap is unthinkable, what could be more rational than a stand-in standing by? Your alternate may be something you've designed especially for just such an emergency, or it may be a piece which, though incredibly complicated in its central design, has reached a submissive backgrounding stage *where you've purposely left it*. Whatever you arrange to have on hand, be certain it's mentally untaxing, heaven to hold, and perfectly easy to pick up or put down at will.

As predicted in the chapter on design, your head is now awash with a lot of good ideas. You've developed a consciousness of what will work in the needlepoint medium, and there's a wellspring of schemes you want to try out before they dry up. Don't hold back because you may already be involved with something else.

Though there's no law against cutting into a new canvas, you've by now collected a nice little cache of leftovers and this is as good a time as any to begin using them. At least one scrap should be exactly right for your first side-line adventure.

If a colorful geometric has been building in your imagination, put it down on graph paper to the size of the canvas you've selected. If you fancy some more natural form and have found a drawing or illustration you'd like to duplicate, have it blown up right away and transfer it to your canvas. I often have several design inspirations photostated at the same time so they'll be on hand and ready to use when I need them.

After you've assembled your wool choices, your prepared canvas and the model you intend to follow, put them into their own private plastic bag. It may be weeks before there's further progress but, when you really need that alternate, it'll be there waiting for the first stitches. There'll never be a frenzied, last-minute crisis, for the worst thing you can do, and one which nearly always ends in grief, is to plan a design in a big hurry because you absolutely must have something to work on immediately. You'll begin to hate what you're doing while you're doing it. When it's finished (if it ever is), you'll hate yourself.

How by-products are born

In illustration of how the magic system works: While I was inching my way across the vast reaches of the Chinese wall panel, a number of lesser productions were brought forth along the way. They were started, finished and found homes, either with me, or someone else (since several were made to be given as gifts), and there was no perceptible break in the ever-forward march of the larger project. In a sense, I never abandoned the panel; the by-products were, indeed, by-products and largely begot in periods when, either I wouldn't, or couldn't have worked on it anyhow.

The strawberry sandals (Fig. 18, after p. 96) were begun when I was involved in the slow process of enlarging the design for my wall hanging and transferring it to canvas. The four little straps were picked up during such oddly scattered minutes that, by now, I scarcely remember completing them.

The shell pillows (Fig. 17, after p. 96) came into being when the panel was more than half finished, but they were tucked into the backs of the pair of chairs beside my fireplace long before the big piece was hanging on the wall. The shells were a good deal more complicated to evolve than the simple strawberries but, to offset their complexity, they're also very small, and I did the modeling during a few evenings when I felt I needed a little holiday from those crazy beasts. The borders are so idiot-easy that, aside from the most elementary counting on one side, they were as anesthetic to stitch as the backgrounds.

The mini Op pillow (Fig. 19, after p. 96) is another proliferation, and you'll note that none of these is either large or important. Two major productions in work simultaneously would be a great mistake. Further, these supplementary pieces were progressed *only* during odd or waiting minutes. You must be entirely disciplined about this. I can't stress strongly enough that there's no other way in which the system can be made to work. If you go compulsive, you've not only missed the point, you're right back with those idle fingers. After all, I wasn't in any really acute need of these little pillows, or the sandals either, for that matter.

All this may seem a sad-commentary on the amount of time we spend just waiting for one thing or another but, on the sunnier side, think how much better it is to add a few stitches to something worth having than to pace the floor and fret or, in the case of those tardy guests, to watch the clock and think about whats drying up in the oven. Your results will be, both boon and bonus, and that's a pretty rewarding double profit.

Traveling needlepoint

No matter what lighthearted pleasures or cultural rewards wait at the end of any journey, getting there is apt to be tiresome, especially if you fly, and that seems to be about the only way to go these days.

You'll do time in wretched airports in order to make connecting flights; planes will almost invariably be delayed and, when you at last strap yourself into your seat, there are interminable hours aloft to be lived through. I don't count these trials among the blessings of travel and, for me, a book isn't an absolute panacea for the restlessness which attacks even before the motors rev for take off. On the other hand, something to read *and* a piece of needlepoint make a journey almost bearable.

You'll often be happy to have something to stitch when you're not in transit too. It can fill a bundle of relaxed, uncharted half hours when you need to rest weary feet or just generally unwind after too much activity.

Follow all instructions for planning and assembling stand-in projects. If your trip is to be a long one, divide your wool. Keep the bulk of it in your main luggage, and carry with your canvas only what you will need to work with for one particular leg of the journey. You don't want to scramble through a lot of colors you haven't time to use.

If you're traveling by ship and are off on a world cruise, by all means take a rug if you like. Otherwise, remember all the rules for avoiding the unwieldly, and the intricate, and give thought to the following suggestions:

Do take a few extra needles, unless you like crawling about on the floor in search of the one you dropped when the stewardess surprised you with the dinner tray.

Do slip a ribbon through the handle of your scissors so you can hook it over your bag strap, your wrist or through a buttonhole. It's easy to forget they're in your lap if you leave your seat.

Do remember to include that emery board with the other essentials.

Don't choose a canvas with too small a mesh count. You won't often find perfect lighting conditions. A 12-count canvas is ideal for traveling needlepoint; 14 is too taxing, and 10 is generally a bad choice for small projects.

Don't take something with you that's nearly finished. You'll be caught empty-handed about halfway through your holiday. If I know a trip is in the offing, I sometimes make a point of progressing a suitable piece of needlepoint to a background-only stage. A simple, one-color area is a magic carpet that takes you where you're going in record time.

Don't be untidy. Put all those snipped ends and picked-out fuzz in a paper cup, or use the waxed bag in the seat pocket ahead as a scrap basket. You don't want your section to look as though you'd been building a nest.

VII

The Thought Counts

An offering of needlepoint is a very personal extension *of* you, but never for a moment forget that it's not *for* you. Carefully tailor whatever you stitch to the tastes, background and preferences of the individual for whom it's intended. What you create will be a labor of love so, before you begin, be reasonably certain the recipient is going to love your labor.

Make your gift a welcome one

If the gift is to be a pillow—and this is a usual and usually useful choice—let's assume you won't needlepoint an identical design in identical colors for the young couple living casually country in a clutter of children, dogs and gerbils, and the woman alone whose address is city, and whose apartment is ultra sleek and carefully polished.

Remember that someone who likes her woods mellowed and her chintzes softly faded isn't going to be enchanted with what you might possibly have invented for a man who's happy with the feel of leather and the glint of steel furniture.

As an extreme example: your good friend Sam is going to have a birthday six weeks from tomorrow and you'd like to needlepoint a present. Sam collects small bronzes, and his digs are done up in total brown from expresso to pale tobacco. Plainly, he's a most conservative fellow so, for heaven's sake, don't make anything with a snappy motif worked in acid yellow, fierce pinks and violets just because you may be taken with the idea of doing something like that at the moment. Perhaps you can save this one for his sister, Samantha, who glitters in an ambiance of lucite, shiny lacquer and just such way-out colors.

Research something like an ancient coin for Sam. Have it blown up, reproduce it on canvas, and you've got it made. He'll absolutely love it. If imagination or sources fail you, stick to a discreet geometric repeat, using Sam's low-key palette, and he'll thank you almost as warmly.

All this advice may seem only basic common sense, but you've no idea how much easier it is to be trapped by inspirational whim when your work is for giving rather than for keeping. Project yourself into the recipient's house, and even into his head, if you want to come up with a perfect gift notion.

If, like Sam, the object of your affectionate stitches is a collector (and who is not these days?) tie up your design with whatever objects he or she is busily amassing. Execute the idea with flair and the result will be cherished as an additional trophy.

The lady with the garden full of flowers will surely welcome a few of her favorites to bloom both in and out of season. Should her taste and activities run more toward the kitchen garden, a fat, white cauliflower or a full-blown lettuce worked in the center of a cushion can be astonishingly beautiful. And don't bypass herbs for the gardener, or for the friend who loves to cook.

When there's no discernable sign of either hobby or acquisition, then you've only color and style to guide you toward a successful gift. If the room is traditional, you're safe with any Florentine or bargello pattern done in appropriate colors. For a more contemporary setting, you may have greater scope, but color will still be your pilot.

The gift of a pillow needn't be confined to the adults on your list of friends. One for a small girl's room can become a quasi-heirloom and be handed down to her own daughter one day. It can be a one-of-a-kind, very special offering to a new baby, though I suggest you start work on this after the fact, when you know which kind of baby it is, and the name that's been chosen. The new-born isn't apt to show much appreciation, but the mother will. Later on—if you haven't gone too baby blue or pink and have given the design some style, there's no reason why the gift shoudn't follow the child through quite a few birthdays. I hope this will be true of the little pillow I made for Sofia, whose birthday and mine fall on the same day (Fig. 20, after p. 96).

Gift ideas

Aside from pillows, which I class as presents of much worth and considerable importance, there are all sorts of smaller things to be made for giving away.

Little purses (larger sizes become consequential again) are delightful to receive and to use. Eyeglass cases are equally acceptable, and can range from delicate ones for evening to whopping big jobs to hold sunglasses. These may be for masculine or feminine use. They can be made to carry about, or to stay put on a bedside table or beside a favorite reading light.

Belts (Fig. 21, after p. 96) make dandy gifts for either sex too (just be sure you have the proper waist measure), and if you come across an attractive old buckle, the gift will be even more appealing. These can often be found if you rummage in shops that carry antique buttons and other such dusty oddments.

If a friend sews her own clothes, design a pair of patch pockets for a jacket. Should you want to go all out with a package deal, buy a remnant of beautiful woolen and do the pockets to blend with the fabric.

Even an entertaining pincushion can become a treasured bit of nonsense and, since you've guarded all those scraps of canvas and leftover bits of yarn, many of the gifts suggested will cost you not a penny. A little time and some careful, loving thought are often just about all you'll need to spend.

It would be too much of a squeeze to put more than the design itself into some of these pocket-sized gifts but, where there's sufficient space, leave room to include your joint initials and, possibly, the date in order to make your offering as personal and special as possible.

* * *

With what appears to be half the total population and virtually all your friends and relations merrily stitching on canvas these days, what of them? Is it back to the scarf counter and the gift department when birthdays and Christmases come round? Not at all. Give the needlepointer needlepoint, by all means. Painters exchange paintings, you know.

I, for one, have gone all misty-eyed when I've unwrapped such a present. Who, after all, is better equipped to measure fully the time, effort, thought and sheer devotion which went into that canvas along with the stitches than another needlepointer? I caution you to work particularly carefully, however. The most appreciative eye won't be able to resist the jeweler's loupe inspection so be prepared.

Unless your style is so distinctive and so unlike that of anyone else, avoid making just another extraneous, albeit beautiful and decorative creation. Try for a little significance and the gift will be twice prized. It isn't mandatory for a sentimental gesture to be either maudlin or banal, so choose an idea that has meaning for the recipient or, even more to the point, for you both.

The strawberry basket (Fig. 22, after p. 96) is an illustration of what I mean. My lady-doctor and friend sent me an especially delightful card last Christmas. It's a reproduction of an anonymous nineteenth-century painting, which we both found enchanting.

For one of my stand-in projects, I isolated the basket, which is only a small portion of the composition, and stitched it as a sort of bread-upon-the-waters gift for her.

While we're on the subject of sentiment, I have one small, cynical word to add. Unless you're quite positive a fancy is more than passing, beware the tender, private joke, or the *semper fidelis* sort of thing worked out in heartbeat red and your monograms inextricably intertwined. You might just be left holding the bag in the shape of a half-finished piece of pretty pointless needlepoint. Unless you're a masochistic ripper, you could find the picking out more painful than the parting.

Whatever you do for giving, remember you'd like your work to be proudly displayed and valued for its many merits. If it's a pillow you've made, you don't want it to live with velvet lining facing front until you ring the door bell. You could have sewed to pieces of velvet together in the first place, and with far less effort.

VIII

How to Cope with Disaster

It is said that the Japanese will make a single, quite intentional error in anything he creates. Perfection is permitted only to his oriental diety, and tradition dictates that no purely mortal artist or artisan may aspire to such a degree of super-excellence.

This not terribly useful bit of knowledge encouraged me to leave my first needlepoint mistake uncorrected. I thought of it as my token. After I'd made three additional flubs within an embarrassingly brief period, I felt the gods had been over-appeased. I also freely admitted I was being far less Japanese than just plain careless so, I did penance. I picked out the fouled-up stitches and promised myself there'd be no more of *that*. Ha!

As proficiency increases, mistakes will naturally diminish but, like germs of the common cold, they'll be around to plague from time to time. A certain amount of picking out seems to be an unavoidable penalty in the needlepoint game, and you may as well face it. I'd like to believe this mortification builds character but, truthfully, it's only a big, fat bore so, before you're instructed in the gentle (and I do mean gentle) art of removing faulty stitches, let me give you some suggestions about how to avoid putting at least a few of them in.

How to avoid mistakes

First of all, never work when you're overtired. By this I do not mean when you're beat from a hard day's labor, or even a hard day's play. That's when needlepoint is most beneficent and soothing. Being weary as a result of needlepointing over too long a stretch is something else again. When your eyes are marshmallows toasting on pointy sticks, when your yarn snarls and so do you, it's time to neatly fold your canvas and go to bed. If it isn't bedtime, take the dog for a long walk, wash your hair, bake an apple strudel. Do anything. Just don't needlepoint.

Skiers warn that you must never take the last run of the day. This, translated, means you'd better stop when you begin to tire—or else. It is true that judgment is faulty when day turns to dusk on the slopes; shadows change shape, bumps smooth out and ruts disappear altogether, but the big ski hazard is fatigue.

While I'm not suggesting that you may break an arm if you don't put your work aside before complete exhaustion sets in, the chance that an accident will befall your tapestry is very good indeed. At best you'll misdirect a few stitches. At worst you'll create a bungle which will take you many tedious hours to undo. Never forget that inattention and carelessness march side by side with weariness. Curiously, you'll invariably find your mistake happened three or four yarn lengths back, and you'll remember it was at this very point you told yourself it was time to knock off.

A switch from thinking to non-thinking needlepoint is another fine method of eliminating a bunch of blunders. Apportion the two according to your mood, your attention span and your patience quota of the moment. When you've burrowed in for a long session with whatever you're currently creating, begin by concentrating on intricate detail, color blending or any complex modeling. Do all the finicky bits you can while you're fresh and both you and your eyes are bright. When inspiration flags, and you find you no longer enjoy mixing the six shades of green in those leaves, change over to a simple, one tone, one stitch, ordinarily tiresome background. What in the initial work stages would create a martyr syndrome, becomes a relaxing, mindless flow of accomplishment. As the area grows and progresses so comfortably, it's also nice to know you're not making any catastrophes along the way.

This rule for intricate versus simple stitchery should apply to periods of social needlepointing as well. Of course you can talk and needlepoint at the same time—if you're among tolerant and understanding friends. You can carry on a perfectly sensible or, perhaps, even a brilliant conversation as you work but, if you're going to continually count stitches, or you've involved yourself in something like the delicate shading of a rose petal, you can forget all about joining discussions concerning geopolitics or the latest controversial film.

It all cooks down to these basic facts. If you don't concentrate on your stitches, that rose petal is going to be a mess. If you give it your entire attention, you're a very rude hostess or guest, as the case may be. In order to keep yourself socially acceptable and your needlepoint neat, work in uncomplicated areas when there are distractions.

This same rule should hold true when you have a limited time to work and not enough for elaborate thinking. If you can only do a few stitches, be very sure you know exactly where to put them.

Obviously you can make an error even in the simplest of backgrounds, but these are easily caught—up to the point of exhaustion, that is. Check back from time to time, just to make certain you haven't skipped a mesh, started a row of basket-weave stitch in the wrong direction, or done something equally untidy.

Don't forget one of the soundest methods for avoiding mistakes. *Find the best of all possible lights in which to work.*

How to correct mistakes

Although I hope they'll help a great deal, none of the foregoing advice can keep your creations totally fault-free. Inevitably, you will make mistakes. Just as inevitably, you will—I hope—correct them.

If you've made your gaff only a minimum number of stitches back, there's not much problem. Simply unthread your needle and insert it under the last stitch you made. Ease the yarn into a small loop and pull it gently back through the mesh. In the same manner, go on to the next stitch, and the next, until you reach the scene of the crime. If you meet with any resistance as you work from the top surface, turn the canvas over and attack from the rear. Remember never to tug hard on your wool, and don't pull or stretch the meshes unnecessarily.

If the row, or portion you're removing has used more than half a thread length, cut it off (after you've anchored it into the surrounding stitches) and retire it. The yarn will be too thin and enfeebled for re-use. If you've only a dozen or so stitches to take out, simply re-thread and forge on.

The big test of character comes when you reluctantly admit that an entire block of design must disappear. To complicate your problem, the disaster area may well be made up of a number of different colors and shades.

Clearly, to remove a section of this sort, you need unflagging perseverance and the skilled, nerveless fingers of a brain surgeon. Your instruments will be the needle again, plus the little embroidery scissors—so sharp, so perilous.

As before, you will begin by slipping your needle under one stitch. This time, lift it high enough so you can actually see the canvas mesh underneath. When you introduce the point of your scissors to snip the yarn, you must be certain it's the wool alone you're cutting. Always advance slowly and cautiously. The sundering of a canvas thread results in more than a surface wound. It's more like a severed artery.

Since it's quite likely these misbegotten stitches haven't followed one another in regular, routine progression, you'll be forced to repeat the snipping process at more or less frequent intervals. Pick out with your needle when possible. When nothing gives, cut.

I know several practiced needlepointers who are devoted to those vicious, razor-sharp hooks dressmakers use for seam ripping. This is a mean little instrument and it absolutely terrifies me. Although I'll stick with the scissors, I mention the ripper because you may find it magical. These can be purchased in any notions department.

As you approach the periphery of the section you're demolishing, stop cutting and use only your needle. You must produce yarn ends sufficiently long to thread into the needle. These you will anchor securely as you would any terminal stitch.

I won't pretend this is anything other than a tiresome ordeal, but the result will give you more than just a lot of woolly fuzz. You'll not only feel exceedingly virtuous, there will be a fine, empty area of canvas which you will rework more thoughtfully.

* * *

If the worst befalls you, and you do cut a canvas thread, don't despair. You can repair the damage satisfactorily enough in one of two ways.

For mending one single snip, pull a short length of canvas thread out of the unworked portion. Hold it in place with the thumb of your left hand and stitch right over it—the thread, that is, not your thumb. If the incision is close enough to the surrounding stitches, you can anchor one end of this thread just as you would do with yarn.

If the injury is more extensive, it will be necessary to make a patch. Cut a piece of canvas from your margin about a half inch larger all round than the area under repair. Make certain the meshes of the patch match the meshes of your canvas precisely, then baste the two loosely together from the wrong side. Work through both thicknesses as though they were one and you'll have done an invisible mend.

There's another variety of fault correction. This one doesn't involve taking out. It's rather more concerned with putting in. I suppose there will be those who question the legality of this trick, but no matter. It's a handy and effective dodge.

When you find there's either not sufficient contrast between two contiguous colors, or you haven't achieved enough tone depth and definition in some accent area, picking out isn't always the inevitable and sole solution. Quite often you can snap up the under-defined spots with a little overstitching, using a shade of either deeper or lighter value.

This method of correction isn't suggested for great fields of stitches. Save the retouching for highlights too low, for shadows too timid, and any small areas where there isn't enough tonal contrast. This overstitching is very much like overpainting in oils, and the result is just about the same.

Don't attempt this job with strands of the same thickness you put into the original stitches. They'll grow too fat, and will be alien to their neighbors.

Separate the plies, and don't mind if you haven't entirely concealed the yarn underneath. The visual end result would be the same had you blended two shades of wool in the first place.

If it seems appropriate, you might sometimes add this zing by using mercerized embroidery floss or silk instead of wool. This will give you contrast of texture as well as color.

Some advice

Don't split your yarn threads as you work. Not only does this careless habit mar the smooth look of your stitches, you'll find yourself hopelessly tangled if you must remove an error. Incidentally, never split your canvas threads.

Don't try to root out a false stitch by putting your threaded needle in reverse through a canvas mesh. This trick may work once in twenty tries. The average isn't worth the double problem you'll create in the nineteen abortive attempts.

Don't fake a misdirected stitch by going over it. You'll never get away with it. Take it out and correct it.

Don't re-use a strand you've ripped out. Taking a thread out weakens it more than putting it in, so throw it away.

Don't needlepoint in anything other than a good light—if you can manage it.

Be sure to cut all anchored threads very short. If you don't, you'll achieve subtle shading where you don't want any shading at all. Especially when you're working in basket weave, it's all too easy for an end to tangle and mingle with the thread you're using.

Sometimes you can leap over a small, unworked space into another area you want to stitch in the same color. Usually, the bridged thread will disappear into the subsequent surrounding stitches. Don't do this with a dark color and cover it with a light one. It will show through after blocking, so better to snip and begin again.

In a large area, if you find your threads are terminating in about the same spot, cut several strands short in order to stagger your beginnings and endings. Better to waste a little wool than to create an unsightly lump.

Proofread your needlepoint very carefully before blocking. Hold it up to a strong light and any small, forgotten segments will show up like eyes in a Halloween pumpkin. To discover one of these six weeks after the piece has been mounted is a shattering experience.

IX

Blocking

Triumph! The last thread has been anchored. Your canvas is finished and ready for the blocking step. Almost.

Before you break out the drawing board and push pins, do a final check-out. Examine your needlepoint carefully. Search for missed stitches and the tiny, unworked corner you thought you'd remember to go back to, and didn't. Look for loose stitches and pull them tight. Clip all trailing yarn ends and, just generally, tidy up.

Now for blocking:

Over the years, I have read a number of instructions about how to begin blocking a piece of completed needlepoint. One set of directions advises that a steam iron is all you need to return a finished piece to its original shape. Others prescribe damping the back of the canvas with a sponge dipped in clear water. A few advocate complete immersion, again in clear water.

In my opinion, the method you choose to employ depends entirely on the state of your canvas. If it hasn't stretched itself into an eccentric rhomboidal figure, the use of a steam iron is a fine idea. The dampness created by the vapor will make the canvas just pliable enough to allow you to make any small, necessary adjustments.

A light sponging followed by stretching is sufficient, too, if your needlepoint is only very slightly distorted but, if the canvas is really misshapen, either because of the way you work, or because of the stitch you've used, a thorough soaking is your only solution.

According to the circumstances and condition of your finished work, any of these methods is correct. I must add that they're correct as far as they go. There are times when none goes far enough.

My fingers, I'm reasonably certain, are no grubbier than the average fingers in this grubby world, and I'm neurotic about washing them when I'm needlepointing. However, I contend it's impossible to labor over a piece of tapestry for X number of weeks or months and end with a pristine, soil-free, immaculate result.

You may be the most compulsive hand-washer in the case books but, if you live in a polluted city (and what city is not?) some grime is bound to fall among your stitches. Picture, for example, a vast wasteland of white background. It's an enormous component of an enormous project which has taken you seven months, seven days and three final, frantic hours to create. No matter how carefully you protected it by rolling and pinning up the finished portions as you worked; no matter how many cakes of soap you dissolved, it cannot possibly end as driven snow.

If you and your needlepoint are traveling together, you can really forget all about that clear water and sponge deal. You will look back on a narrow grayish strip and remember the hour and fifteen minutes you spent in the Valencia airport waiting for a plane to Barcelona. The somewhat dusty carnation among the clean pink ones flowered, you'll recall, aboard the Rapido speeding from Rome to Florence. It's one way of keeping a travelog, but I'd stick to snap shots and a note book if I were you.

Instructions

So, whether at home or abroad, it seems pretty evident there are times when a little more than clear water and a sponge is required. You will, in fact, need soap.*

If the gentle-acting liquids sold for washing delicate woolens are good enough for cashmere sweaters, I figure they're good enough for my needlepoint, which is considerably tougher.

Follow the directions on the bottle. These usually specify a capful of soap to a hand-basin of lukewarm water.

Let the piece soak for some minutes, and knead it tenderly a few times. Rinse well, then press out as much water as possible. Never twist or wring the needlepoint. Now, roll it firmly in a turkish towel, just as you would a sweater. If it's a fairly large piece, I suggest you use a whole lot of towels. The more moisture you can manage to get rid of, the faster the drying process will be.

If soap wasn't necessary, and you wet the canvas only to reshape it, you'll employ this same blotting procedure.

If your needlepoint has been made for something with a definite shape—like a chair seat, for example—you will have kept a paper pattern. Use this as your guide, and follow the outline as you stretch the piece back into its original form.

*In all the needlepoint books I've read, only Mary Martin's matter of factly directs, "Wash the needlepoint—"

BLOCKING

When the project is a simple square or rectangle, unless it's been designed to fit something so specific that a fraction of an inch is important, I prefer to lay the needlepoint on a turkish towel. This flattens the wool less than the ungiving surface of brown paper on board, and my plastic triangle serves to true the sides and corners as effectively as a ruled guideline would do.

Whichever surface you choose, brown paper or bath towel, place it on your drawing board, then lay your damp and very relaxed canvas, right side down, on top. Pat the needlepoint into place until it more or less conforms to shape.

Now, armed with your tack hammer, begin tapping in your pushpins. Do not put them through your stitches. Place them about a half inch out into the unworked margin and, let me remind you again, they *must* be rustproof.

A properly blocked needlepoint should look like this. All scalloped edges and unwanted curves should be gently eased straight. The rustproof tacks should never be removed before the needlepoint is thoroughly dry. Even if only slightly damp the needlepoint will spring out of shape and the whole blocking process will have to be done over.

Start with the outermost corners, then divide and subdivide the spaces in between—top and bottom, side and side as illustrated here, until your pins are about a half inch apart. Pat, stretch and continually adjust as you tack until all your edges are straight and true. The larger the piece, or the more distorted, the more difficult the job will be, but take your time. You don't want to repeat this maneuver.

When you're quite satisfied with this reconstruction, I suggest you go away and forget about your project for a while. Depending on the weather, the amount of heat in your house and the weight of the wool you used, the piece should remain undisturbed for from twenty-four to thirty-six hours—more if the weather is really rotten. Don't be in a hurry to look upon this miracle you've wrought. If the needlepoint isn't dry as bones, it'll snap right back into its old misshapen shape. The exposed side may feel dry to the touch within a few hours, but don't be misled. It isn't.

And a word of warning; never try to hasten the action by putting the stretched canvas near heat. Your wool will harden and your work will be utterly ruined.

After you're certain the piece is thoroughly dry, pull out the tacks. You'll find all the starch has returned to the canvas and it will be stiff as new. Now, place a turkish towel over your ironing board and lay the needlepoint on it, again face down. Hold a steam iron just above it, and not quite touching. This steaming will restore your wool to its original bouncy state, and the slight moisture you create will make it possible to adjust any little scallop which may have resulted from tacking.

These instructions will serve you well for any small to average-sized undertaking or, to be more specific, anything no larger than your drawing board. Should you have space in the back of a closet, or behind the sofa for a big piece of plywood, your blocking can be more ambitious but, if the project is sizable, be prepared to call in some extra hands to help you heave ho. You won't be able to manage the stretching all alone, so don't try.

When you've made something as large as a rug, you'll have no choice other than to leave the blocking to a professional expert. By all means get estimates for the job, but have no doubt that you've chosen someone both reliable and proficient. The stitches you will put into his hands are very precious.

Equipment for blocking

DRAWING BOARD: This should be the largest size you can purchase in an art supply store. You may want to substitute a large piece of plywood. Keep both on hand if you have space.

DRAWING PINS: These are also called pushpins. Do not use thumbtacks. The drawing pins are aluminum and they're rustproof. Buy a big box.

TRIANGLE: Buy the transparent plastic kind in a medium size. Better still, equip yourself with two sizes. They aren't very expensive.

All the above has been previously specified in Chapter II. These will serve a dual purpose. In addition:

LIQUID SOAP: Buy the best name brand made for washing fine woolens.

STEAM IRON: Should you not own a steam iron, you can improvise. Lay a dampened cloth over your needlepoint, and hold an ordinary dry iron just above it. You'll get the same result.

TOWELS: Presumably you have these in your linen closet. Don't be miserly with them.

FIGURE 17 Two small shell pillows.

FIGURE 18 Two different sandal designs made from left-over canvas.

FIGURE 19 Another stand-in to work on when it's too inconvenient to pick up or bring along that large project.

FIGURE 20 Sophia's pillow.

FIGURE 21 A belt designed in needlepoint is an appreciated and thoughtful gift.

FIGURE 22 From a more complex design I isolated and copied this strawberry basket to make a charming pillow for a friend.

FIGURE 23 Needlepoint for chair back in progress. Notice the pattern outline on the canvas, as well as the vertical and horizontal center guidelines.

FIGURE 24 The leftover piece of canvas can be turned into a very chic pocket flap.

X

Mounting

My approach to this chapter is somewhat apprehensive for, while there are, indeed, some needlepoint pieces which can be brought to a state of completion by your own hand—and successfully—the number is limited. Pitfalls of abyss-like depths wait to swallow up your beautiful stitches if you try to do it yourself, and most final operations are best left to the expertise of a professional. He may not know a thing about doing needlepoint, but he does know his own craft.

Upholstering should be left to the man who knows how to upholster and has all the necessary tools within reach. As for rugs, unless you've made quite a small one, the finishing (especially the blocking) will be impossible for the amateur to manage.

A bag maker should make up anything more complicated than the simplest envelope purse (he'll really do a better job on that too), and I'd be totally dishonest if I suggested you could learn to tap out a pair of sandals on your own little cobbler's bench.

By and large, mounting your own needlepoint is tricky and dangerous. Don't experiment. You won't save a nickle by turning out a clumsy bungle. If it's possible to salvage it, you'll still pay for the professional job. Sometimes your work can be botched beyond saving, and all you'll have left is a lesson painfully learned.

Instructions

Now that I've struck fear into your very heart and soul, I shall proceed with instructions for finishing several projects. You really *can* do these all alone—and be proud of the results, besides.

PILLOWS   Putting together a pillow is a job your upholsterer can, and most gladly will do for you—at a staggering price. However, the operation is a relatively simple one and, if you make a whole lot of pillows, you'll save a whole lot of money. Believe me, the amount is bedazzling.

To begin at an essential beginning, you should purchase the insides of your pillow before you start the needlepoint. Most department stores carry ready-filled cases and, while these come in a number of different sizes, they don't come in *every* size, so it's best to let them dictate the dimensions of your needle-point area. The ideal stuffing is down. This is the most luxurious material you can use, but it's also the most costly. Casings filled with foam rubber bits or other commercial substances won't actually disgrace your work if you wish to spend a lot less.

Whatever you use, just be certain it's *in* an inside casing. Don't stuff wads of wool or cotton batting into your pillow. This is unprofessional and lumpy, besides. An exception must be made for the mini pillow you've done from a canvas scrap. Since you'd never find anything ready-made to fit, just fill it neatly with lamb's wool.

Not long ago, I needlepointed a pillow for one of my step-daughters which, because of customs, duties and other overseas difficulties, was empty of anything except apology and an explanation. When she wrote to say how pleased she was, she added that she'd stuffed it with discarded pantyhose. This is one way, I suppose, but I think I'd stick to filled casings.

After your needlepoint has been blocked and dried, the next thing to think about is the backing. A number of different fabrics are possible, but be sure your choice is worthy of the stitches up front. It should be elegant, of course, but it must be sturdy as well. Velvets are always an excellent material—not thin dress velvets, but those used for upholstery with cotton or, preferably, linen backs. A smooth wool is nice for backing, and a really heavy, closely woven silk will work well too.

The color you choose will blend with the needlepoint, but think of pillows to come when you select the backing. When you buy a half yard of wool or velvet, you'll have a strip 54 inches long—enough for three large pillows, or a number of smaller ones. Incidentally, it's a fine idea to glance at remnant counters as you pass by. You often can find fabulous fabric ends which, bought off the bolt, would be outrageously costly.

So, now you find yourself with another little cache of leftovers. I keep mine folded in a box and, more often than not, I find what I need right there, without having to shop for it.

Cut your lining selection at least a half inch larger all around than the size of your needlepointed area. Make sure the material is straight with the grain on all sides. This is important. Draw threads to be absolutely certain.

Lay needlepoint and fabric face-to-face (wrong sides out) on a table, and pin the two together. Next you will baste, but leave a section open to within an inch or so of the corners—at the *bottom* of the pillow.

MOUNTING 103

If, as suggested on page 67, you want to put tassels in the corners, now is the time to think about that. As you pin lining and needlepoint together, pin the yarn ends in each corner, leaving the tassels *inside*. When you turn your pillow right side out, they'll be where they belong.

You could complete the final stitching entirely by hand, I suppose. Careful backstitches put in with heavy linen thread would do the job, but I'm afraid you'd find it a long and laborious operation. I hope you own a sewing machine.

You'll stitch with the needlepoint side up—slowly and meticulously. The needle must pass within the last mesh at the very edge of the needlepointed area. In other words, between the final border stitch and the last thread as shown in the diagram. All sight of white canvas will be eliminated. Don't try to race your machine. Inch it along.

Before you do any trimming of excess canvas and fabric, turn the pillow to check it out. If you've gone out of bounds anywhere, just restitch that section.

Now, you're ready for trimming, *except at the opening you left, and an inch to right and left on either side.* Cut off excess margins to no less than three or four canvas meshes. Lop off a bit of the points at each corner and, before you turn the pillow to the right side, press the flap of fabric at the opening so it's firmly creased. Do the same at the stitch line on the needlepoint side, and you'll have a neat placket to sew by hand.

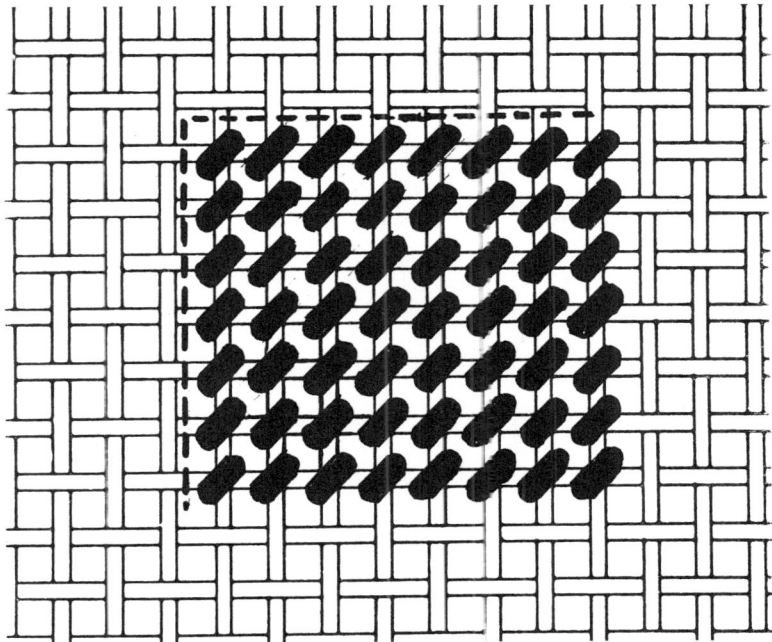

When sewing the pillow needlepoint design to its backing, the machine stitches should be placed between the edge of the stitches and the beginning of the next row of mesh.

After your pillow is right side to, gently poke out the corners so they're as squared as possible. Use something not too sharply pointed—a letter opener is usually good. And I like to press along the edges (on the lining side) with the steam iron so they're neatly knifed.

When you've inserted the inner pillow, slip-stitch the opening together, give your completed work an affectionate smack or two, and it's yours to admire—every stitch.

SLIP SEATS   If the inner construction is in good condition, covering this type of seat is a cinchy job for the amateur upholsterer. If it's collapsed in the middle, or the stuffing has become a musty, matted mess, you'd be wise to let a pro take over. However, you'll have removed the seat from its frame in order to make a preliminary pattern for your design so, in order to simplify these instructions, we'll assume you investigated and found the insides in perfect health.

When you've drawn your outline (and this is important if the seat is shaped), take into consideration the fact that the area you'll needlepoint will be a good deal larger. It must travel over the edges and under the seat for tacking, so provide ample material to be worked with later on. Draw a piece of muslin over the seat in order to determine just how much canvas to cut.

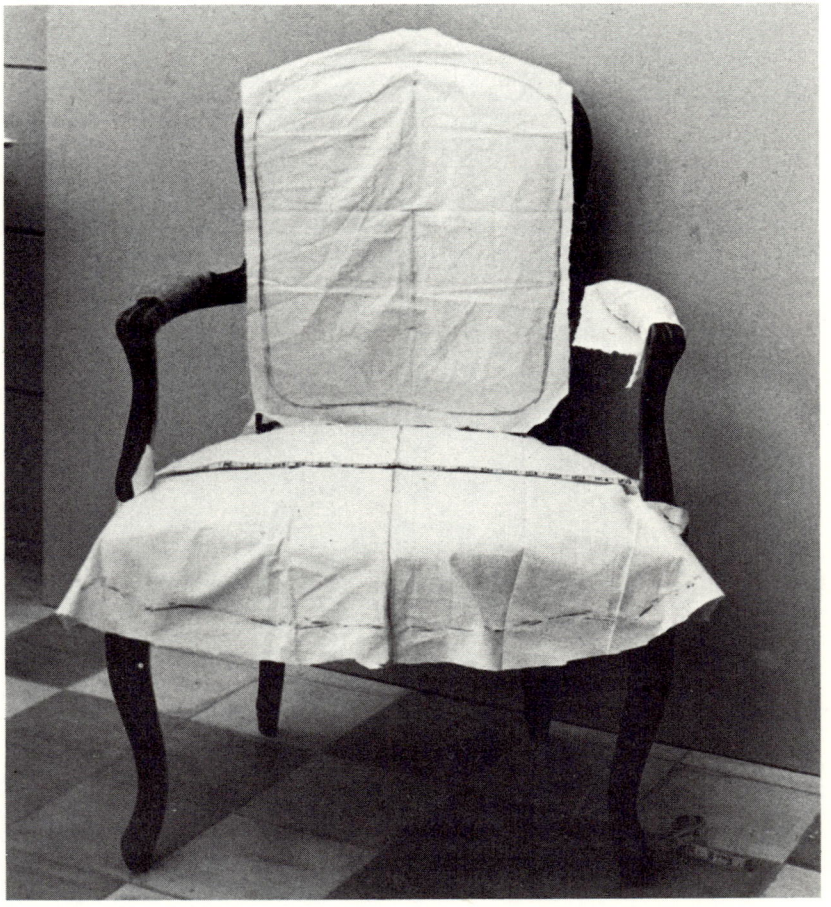

A muslin pattern is made of the seat, back and arms in order to determine the amount of canvas to cut.

When your needlepoint is finished and has been blocked, place it over the seat in the proper position. Check and double check the horizontal and vertical center guidelines to make certain you're on target. Pin through the needlepoint and into the seat itself here and there, using long, straight pins. These will prevent the covering from going askew when you turn the seat over.

Find a sturdy table for the tacking operation and, from my own experience, thumbtacks work best here. Don't push them in too firmly, however, until you're entirely satisfied with your stretching job. With the seat upside down on your table, fold front and back pieces of excess canvas toward the center and over the side sections. Put a tack in each fold and one in between. The corners will be squared off at first, but you'll gradually ease these into little pleats and folds to conform to the shape of the seat—unless it's a simple square or rectangle. A square corner will remain a square corner.

Keep all folds and tucks as flat and neat as you can. If you've more bulk in one section than in another, the seat won't sit properly within its frame.

When the needlepoint is taut and smoothed over the edges to your satisfaction, you'll tack a muslin lining over the bottom. Cut this a little larger than the seat and turn it under all around to make it fit. This you will tack in place with the smallest carpet tacks placed quite close together.

LOOSE CUSHIONS Unless you're faced with a complicated shape, putting a loose seat cushion together isn't any more involved than making a pillow. You will, in fact, follow the same directions for sewing fabric back to needlepoint front.

Should you find it necessary to cut out corners to fit around back and arm supports, you have something more complex to engineer. The bamboo chair with muslin pattern is an example of this problem. If you're not prepared to be unerringly accurate, I'd avoid this struggle. Although it's not an impossibly difficult job, you must be absolutely painstaking.

Once you've drawn the shape of your chair seat on the canvas, with allowance of supports outlined, it's a good idea *not* to follow the shapes of the openings too carefully. Make them smaller—never larger than you've indicated.

Your backing, on the other hand, will be cut precisely, and the stitch lines around the nicks marked with tailor's chalk. You'll see why, later.

The pinning and basting process will follow the usual course. Remember to leave your opening at the back.

Stitch all long, straight edges from the needlepoint side. Leave the nicks and notches undone. Turn the cushion over and stitch these from the fabric side, following the marked guidelines. You will be stitching through needlepoint, so before you do any trimming, turn the cushion and make a trial fitting—just to be sure.

Whether the shape is simple or eccentric, you will buy inch-thick foam rubber for filling (it comes in sheets). Use your pattern again, and cut the piece to conform exactly to finished size. Insert, and slip-stitch the placket.

You'll very likely want to anchor the cushion to chair or bench with tasseled cords. If you don't do this, the cushion will spend a good part of its life on the floor. Directions for making tassels will be found on page 66, and for cords, on page 63.

Sew the flat side of the cord to the edge of the cushion by hand. It's good insurance to go around twice. There will be some strain, and you won't want the cord constantly popping loose.

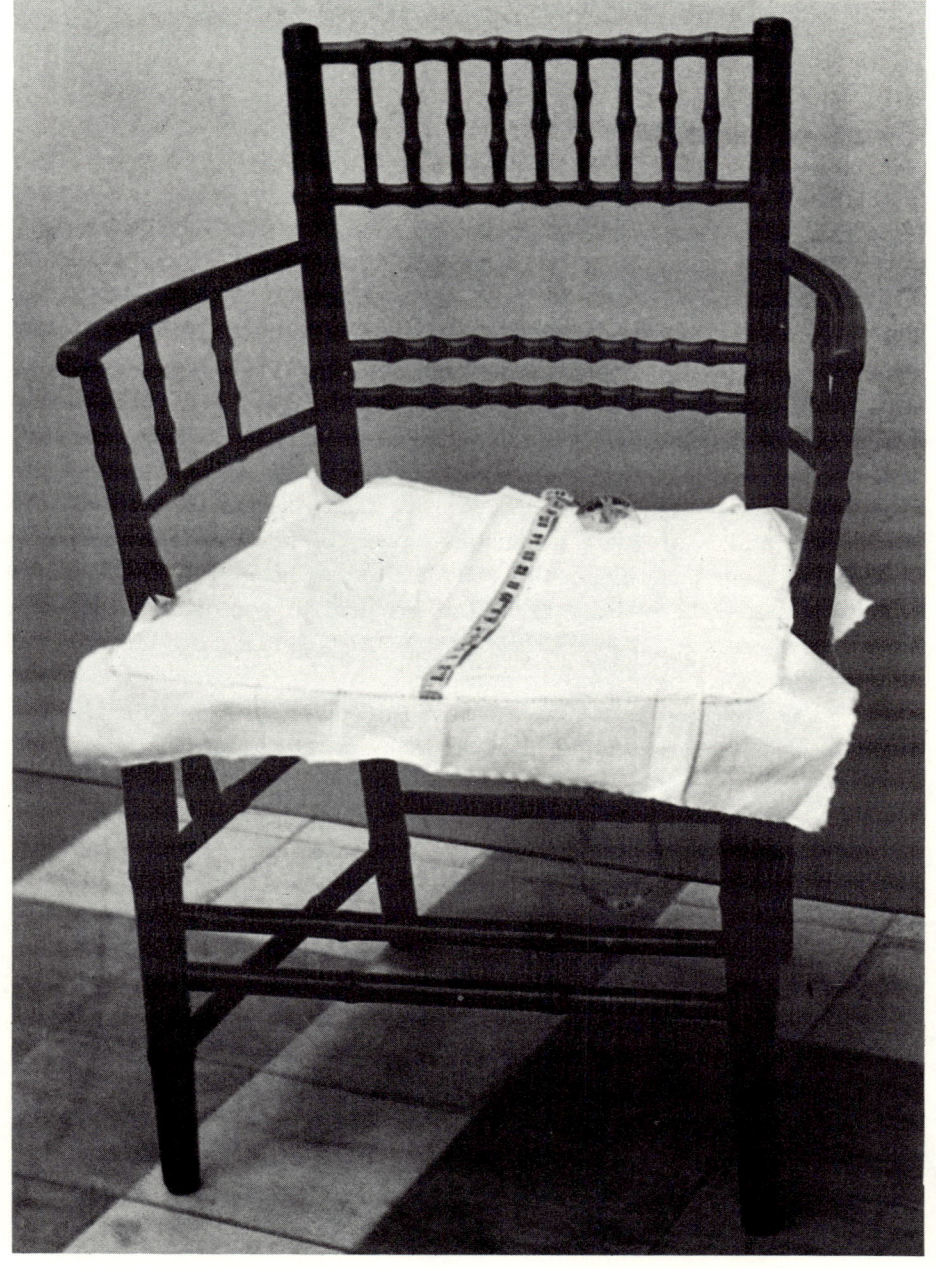

Making a muslin pattern of a seat with fitted corners is more difficult and should not be undertaken unless you're prepared to be painstakingly thorough.

RUGS   I'm being a repetitive bore with the following advice, but do take me seriously. Put the blocking and finishing of any rug larger than 4 by 5 feet into the hands of a professional. Don't even think of attempting the job yourself.

If you wish to block only a very small rug, you'll obviously need something larger than your drawing board for stretching even a 2 by 3. Keep a plywood panel on hand, as suggested in Chapter IX.

You will also require a sturdy assistant to pull while you haul. Remember that both rug wool and rug canvas are harder, heavier and, therefore, more difficult to manipulate. Add the fact of the increased weight to a larger than usual area of stitches, and you'll begin to understand the troubles and struggles ahead.

Assuming that each problem has been faced, and all obstacles overcome, you'll place your blocked, dry, pressed rug upside down on a flat surface. Turn back the unworked margin of canvas on the last line of your needlepoint stitches: pin at intervals and miter the corners.

Slip-stitch the canvas to needlepoint loosely, catching only the barest surface of your woolen stitches.

For the remainder of the finishing operation, I must tell you there are two schools. One believes in lining rugs; the other in binding. I'm a faculty member of the binding school. I eschew linings for myself, and I've always advised against them when I've ordered needlepoint rugs for clients.

Doubtless a lining gives the wrong side of a rug a more finished and luxurious look, but I'm more concerned about what happens on the right side.

That dark space between rug and lining makes a peachy home for moths and carpet beetles. That's the number one hazard. Besides, unless we play Japanese and remove our shoes at the threshold, a certain amount of grit will be well ground into and through the stitches, where it will stay trapped within the lining—even through cleanings. Sharp particles will eventually cut the wool, creating a number two hazard of some importance.

So, my counsel is to bind. Carpet binding is sold by the roll usually, and is very inexpensive. Slip-stitch this tape to the far edge of your unworked canvas. Miter these corners too, then slip-stitch the free side to the back of the rug itself. Even without a lining, your finish will be neat and tidy.

A thin sheet of rubber should be put under your rug if it's to live on a bare floor. It will prolong the life of the rug; it will keep it from rippling and, much more important, it will eliminate accidents caused by slipping, since the rubber hugs both floor and rug.

The rubber padding can be purchased in any department store rug department. It comes in any width and will be delivered ready-cut to your specifications.

CORNICES   The simpler the style of your cornice, the easier it will be to cover, if you plan to do the job yourself. If you don't, your needlepoint design should be more important than architectural detail, anyway.

As suggested in Chapter V, have your carpenter or cabinetmaker construct the cornice box of quarter-inch plywood before you begin to stitch. Tell him the depth you have in mind, but let *him* take the measurements of your windows. If the cornice doesn't quite fit. he'll be responsible for the correction of any errors. He won't be able to blame you. You'll discover that my faith in the dependability of these noble craftsmen is not unqualified. This is the result of long experience and close contact.

Should you have a husband who's handy with saws and things, you're in luck, but I'd still insist that he take his own measurements.

The fewer jigs and jogs put into the structural design, the better, and a straight strip as indicated here is really preferable, for you won't get into trouble when you apply the needlepoint. However, if the design suits your windows, and you feel up to the additional effort, you might have a go at the model with simple side flanges.

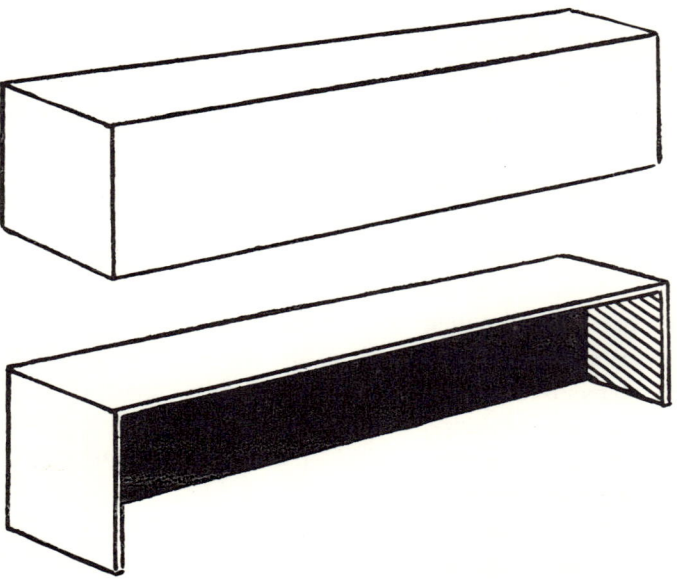

Front and back construction of basic rectangular plywood cornice box. This is scaled to 12 inches deep for a window 40 inches wide and approximately 7 feet high.

If you're unsure about depths and proportions, make a brown paper strip and pin it across your window. If it seems either skimpy or overpowering, it's easy to try other patterns until you're satisfied.

NOTE   Either of these cornices may be constructed without a top enclosure, but these serve as dust caps, and will help keep your curtains or draperies cleaner in this far from immaculate world.

Depth of your cornice will depend entirely on the proportions of your window

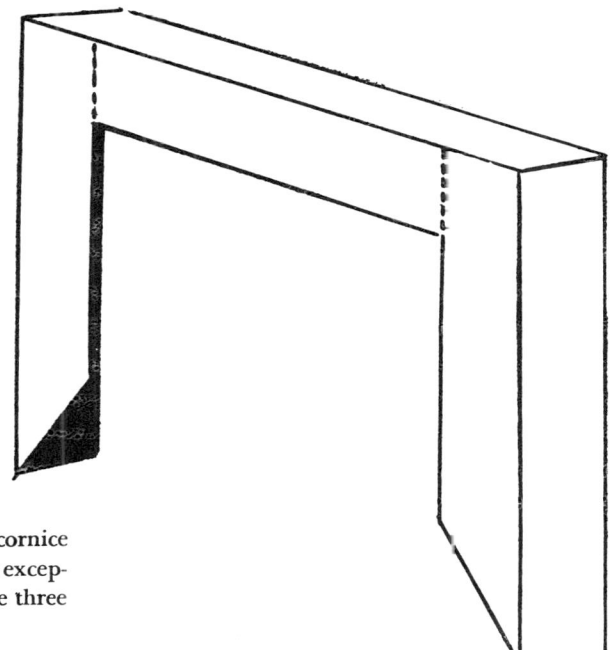

This diagram shows the shape of a cornice with side flanges. Unless this is to fit an exceptionally small window, I suggest you make three sections of needlepoint. See dotted lines.

but, generally speaking, it shouldn't be less than 8 inches nor more than 13 inches.

With all these decisions behind you, the job of upholstering a cornice can be accomplished satisfactorily with small carpet tacks and a tack hammer, but a staple gun is a boon for this and many other projects. A stapler is rather expensive so, unless you plan to use it often enough to amortize the investment, borrow one if you can.

Whether you tack or staple, you'll begin to work at the top of the cornice box. Match the center of your needlepoint to the center of the box. Fold the last two or three rows of stitches over the top and tack into the unworked margin. Keep this line of stitches even as you work outward from the middle to the corners. When you reach these corners, miter the canvas. Continue to tack around the short side sections, then draw the canvas around to the back and tack. Try to keep the last row of stitches right at the very edge of the side front. In other words, don't let them travel around the back if you can avoid it; there will be less bulk when the cornice is installed.

Now, lay the cornice on its face, and again check center marks. Draw the bottom edge of the needlepoint up, over the bottom edge of the box and around to the inside. Tack along the front length, through the unworked canvas always. Work as before—center to ends. Investigate what's going on on the right side frequently. You may be stretching your design unevenly and into some crazy bias.

When you turn the bend at the corners, ease the material into neat pleats and, since it's impossible to tack here, use Elmer's Glue-All. A couple of drawing pins will hold everything until it dries and adheres. You can then finish the short side sections.

In the interests of dust-proofing as well as neatness, it's a good idea to tack a muslin strip across the top, just to the edge of your stitches, and another around the inside. Turn in the edges of the muslin neatly before you tack.

Your finished cornice will be installed with angle irons and screws. Unless you understand this sort of thing, or have that clever husband who knows his way around with drills and bits, you'd better call your friend the carpenter back.

Should you want to hang curtains within the box, telephone a draper instead. He'll cut and secure the proper rods inside, and will install the cornice for you too. Further, if you have faith in the draper, and all this covering process defeated you, turn that over to him as well. The stitches and the design will still be yours alone.

BLOCK TABLES Before you begin needlepointing the panels for your table, the actual wooden block should be in your possession. For this project, the finished covering must *fit*—like skin; not too tight, not too loose. To be sure, you've given all the dimensions to the cabinetmaker, but play it safe.

What you will have—cube or oblong—will not really be a block, since blocks are solid. It will, instead, be a hollow, closed box. Specify a good, paint-grade wood. Insist on no knot holes and no warps. Take a firm stand on carefully joined and smoothly sanded edges.

You will have made five needlepoint panels—four for the sides; one for the top. When these are blocked to *exact* dimensions, pin the side sections together. Baste closely and firmly with small stitches so that your matched meshes will stay matched. Stitch the seams, guiding your needle between last needlepoint stitch and the adjoining canvas thread (see instructions in this chapter for pillows). Sew only the needlepointed portion—let the unworked canvas flaps stay free. This will facilitate attaching the top panel.

Press the seams open and catch-stitch them to the back of the needlepoint so they'll remain open. You have now created something that looks very much like a needlepointed roller towel.

Next, pin one side of the top section to one of the side panels. Again, baste with infinite care. Right angle must meet right angle with perfect precision or all is lost. Stitch and proceed to the opposite side, then to the ones in between. The production has become a rather collapsed, slightly surreal facsimile of a box.

When you've stitched all around, check the corners for any small gaps. It may be necessary to reinforce with a few hand stitches. In fact, it's a good idea even if everything seems secure—these corners will have to take a good deal of stress.

Trim excess canvas at the corners to within a safe number of meshes. Press the remaining seams back and catch-stitch them as you did those on the side portions. Eliminate all the lumps you possibly can. Those inside seams must be neat.

You may prefer another method of joining the panels. Work from the right side with this one, and sew all seams entirely by hand. Turn back the unworked canvas on a line with the last, exposed mesh thread. Lash the pieces together with heavy carpet thread, matching mesh for mesh as always.

You will have a white outline all around, and this you will cover with half-cross stitches, using a yarn to match the needlepointed area. Slant your stitches in the direction of those along the edges.

When you're satisfied with the soft box, slip it over the rigid one and adjust to fit. When all corners and angles jibe, turn your table upside down. Tack, or staple the excess canvas at the bottom and miter the corners. Cut either a piece of felt or vinyl to size, and glue it to the bottom.

Purchase four protective metal domes and attach them to the four bottom corners. These can be found in any hardware store and are called Domes of Silence.

Your beautiful table is finished and almost ready for use. Before you put anything on top, have a piece of glass cut to fit. Tell the glazier to polish all edges.

Should you have any question concerning the wisdom of my advice about taking this precaution, check back to the warnings on page 78.

TABLE TOPS   For this project, you can dispense with the services of carpenter or cabinetmaker. Simply find a handy lumberyard and ask them to cut a piece of plywood to your specifications.

Taking into consideration the thickness of the needlepoint, the dimensions of your top should be approximately $\frac{1}{8}$ inch less on all sides than the size of the surface over which it is to be placed.

The thickness of the plywood panel will depend on the effect you wish to achieve. If you want to duplicate a *trompe l'oeil* slab of marble, for instance, order the wood $\frac{1}{2}$ inch thick. For a less realistically duplicated effect, $\frac{1}{4}$ inch will do nicely.

If you do choose $\frac{1}{2}$-inch thickness, leave little unworked squares in the corners of your canvas. For a neater finish, these can be tucked in and boxed. With a thinner panel, the needlepoint can be drawn over the corners, and no folds or pleats will mar the illusion of a solid surface.

After the needlepoint has been blocked, and if you have left unworked corners, box these by hand. Catch the meshes into a gusset on the wrong side, using carpet thread. You'll have only a few stitches to contend with, but make the joining as invisible as possible. Clip off a small triangle of canvas to eliminate bulk underneath—but not too close.

Put the needlepoint face down on a clean, solid surface and place the plywood on top. Measure all around to see that it's directly in the middle, and match center guidelines which you will have indicated on the plywood surface.

Beginning at the center on each side, draw the needlepoint around to what is now the top side of the wood, and tack or staple. If the area of your table top is sizable, you may need a little assistance. Progress from centers to corners. You will miter the unworked canvas margin as usual. Don't forget to check the true front side from time to time to see whether you're pulling unevenly. Do this especially if your design has any sort of border.

It's all as simple as that. Turn to top face up, and place it where it belongs. Just don't forget the glass top.

WALL HANGINGS   These may be of any size and nearly any dimension—square, plain rectangle or a long, narrow shape which you can design to hang horizontally or vertically. Just don't make it too dinky or too dainty. Allow it to speak.

Blocking difficulties will equal those you'd face had you made a small rug. The size of your blocking problem will correspond exactly with the size of the panel, so simply follow rug instructions.

All steps will be identical until you reach the lining versus binding question. Here you will line.

Buy a decent fabric for lining. It needn't be very heavy, nor luxurious, nor expensive. Find one that blends with the needlepoint and is nice enough to stand inspection should someone flip over a corner after the panel is hung.

Cut the material an inch larger all around than the finished needlepointed area. Draw threads to insure straight, true edges. Turn under the inch allowance, pin and baste, smoothing the fabric as you go along. All this is important because you'll want no bags and swags on the back.

Slip-stitch the edges of the lining just inside the edge of your canvas—but not beyond. It mustn't show from the front. Remove the basting threads and press lightly (on the wrong side, of course) with the steam iron.

Sew three or more metal curtain rings to the back at the top of the panel, but far enough below the edge to be invisible when it's on the wall. Run a curtain rod through the rings. This will hold the tapestry taut for, if you've more than two feet in width, hanging from the rings alone will scallop the top most unattractively.

You may, instead, stitch a strip of the same material to the top of your lining to form a "sleeve" to hold a curtain rod. Turn in the raw edges of a 1½ inch strip to the width of the finished panel. Baste this to the lining, an inch from the top and from either side. Stitch (or sew firmly by hand), leaving one end open to receive the rod. Proceed with the application of lining to needlepoint as per the preceding instructions. With this method, you will be certain a large panel will remain taut forever. Instead of using picture hooks for hanging as you would with rings, drive three nails in the wall. The encased rod will simply rest on these.

It is not by chance alone that all the foregoing instructions are concerned with adornment of your house rather than your person.

With a great many years in the world of interior design behind me, these are projects I understand. I know how they should be put together, and that my directions are practically workable. I know, too, how your achievements will look when they're finished. I can visualize them in your house, and share your pride in having made them yourself.

Conversely, I have never made a purse, nor have I even seen one in the process of being made professionally. It would, therefore, be presumptuous if I tried to tell you how.

I adore hand-made things, but I do not adore them when they're stamped "home-made." Once a considerable amount of thought has been expended on a design, and endless needlepoint stitches have been stitched into what is intended to be a bag, a piece of luggage, or a pair of sandals, the end product should have a sleekly slick, professional look.

I can do plain and, sometimes, rather fancy sewing and I've no doubt I could put together a simple purse not *too* clumsily, but the question is—would I carry it?

In my opinion, the gores, gussets, darts, welts and crisp boxing should be put in with finesse. Skillful stitches must be made by a master hand on machines designed to do the job.

Patch pockets and pocket flaps (Fig. 24, after p. 96) are nothing more than diminutive, unfilled pillows, and are just as easy to make. Sew them to coat or jacket with firm hand stitches.

A belt works on the same principle (though I do advise the addition of stiffening between belt and lining). Keep the closing device as uncomplicated as possible. Heavy hooks and eyes are fine. Place these just inside the edges of the belt ends, so they won't show. Lacings through metal grommets are good, too, especially for a wide belt. Your local shoe repair man will put in the grommets, and you can make a cord, or buy something ready-made in a trimming department. Tie knots in the cut ends, or dip them in Elmer's Glu-All to prevent raveling.

Farther than this I cannot take you along the fashion accessory path. You must read other books to learn the secrets of clutch purses, book covers and something which is invariably called a tote bag. For my own toting, I prefer a nice paper shopping bag, or I did—now, local straw baskets serve me very well.

How to restore your needlepoint

When, alas, the day comes and your needlepoint begins to lose its original fresh look of youth, brighten it up by using a good, foam-type upholstery cleaner. Follow directions, and it'll work minor wonders.

Dry cleaning, for some reason, just doesn't do a thing for needlepoint stitches.

Bibliography

NEEDLEPOINT by Hope Hanley—Scribners

NEW METHODS IN NEEDLEPOINT by Hope Hanley—Scribners

NEEDLEPOINT DESIGN by Louis J. Gartner, Jr.—William Morrow

NEEDLEPOINT BY DESIGN by Maggie Lane—Scribners

SYLVIA SIDNEY NEEDLEPOINT BOOK by Sylvia Sidney—Van Nostrand Reinhold

MARY MARTIN'S NEEDLEPOINT by Mary Martin—William Morrow

BARGELLO by Elsa S. Williams—Van Nostrand Reinhold

FLORENTINE EMBROIDERY by Barbara Snook—Scribners

NEEDLEPOINT FOR EVERYONE by Mary Brooks Picken and Doris White—Harper & Row

Index

Accent colors, 71
Armchairs. *See* Chairs

Bargello (Williams), 57, 114
Basket, as gift, 87
Basket-weave stitch, 43-48
Bellpulls, 79
Belts
   finishing, 113
   as gifts, 86-87
   leftover canvas for, 16
Benches, 76
   designing, 37-38
Bias tent (basket-weave) stitch, 43-48
Bibliography, 114
Black, avoiding, 70
Blocking, 95-99
Borders, 61
Braid trim, 62-63
Bricks, 79
Brick stitch, 50-53

Canvas, 1-9
   cut thread in, 92
   how to buy, 4-5
   how to prepare, 8-9
   leftover, 16-17
   mono, 3
   Penelope, 4
   plan before cutting, 5-8
   types and uses, 1-4
Cat and Fish design, 25-27
Chairs, 76. *See also* Pillows and cushions; Seats
   utilizing canvas for, 7-8
Color, 69-72
   choosing, 69-70
   combining, 71-72
   wool, 70-71
Continental stitch, 48-50
Cords, 63-65
Cornices, 76
   mounting, 107-10
Cotton floss, 11

Crewel wool, 11
Cushions. *See* Pillows and cushions

Decorating with needlepoint, 73-79
   ideas and inspirations, 74-75
   projects, 75-79
Decoupage, 28
Designs, 19-39
   finding, 20-21
   lettering, 23-24
   materials for, 22-23
   method 1, 25-33
   method 2, 33-35
   method 3, 35-36
   painting canvas, 36
   rug, 30-33
   signature, 23
Diagonal (basket-weave), stitch, 43-48
Drawing boards, 22
   for blocking, 98
Drawing pins. *See* Pins

Embroidery floss, 11
Emery boards, 17
Equipment. *See* Tools and equipment

Filoselle silk, 12
Firescreens, 79
Flame stitches, 55-57
   designing with, 39
Florentine Embroidery, 114
Florentine family of stitches, 53
Fly design, 27-28
Frames, 78-79

Gartner, Louis J., Jr., 114
Gifts, 85-88
Glue, to finish canvas, 8
Gobelin stitch, 53-55

Handbook of Ornaments, 24
Hangings. *See* Wall hangings
Hanley, Hope, 114
Headboards, 76
Hemming canvas, 8-9
Herringbone stitch, 57

Irons, steam, 99

Lane, Maggie, 78, 114
Left-handedness, 46
Light, color and, 71
Loose cushions. *See* Pillows and cushions

Martin, Mary, 114
Mary Martin's Needlepoint, 114
Masking tape, to finish canvas, 8
Mistakes, 89-93
   advice on, 93
   avoiding, 90-91
   correcting, 91-93
Monograms and Ciphers, 24
Mounting, 101-12

Needlepoint (Hanley), 114
Needlepoint by Design, 78, 114
Needlepoint Design (Gartner), 114
Needlepoint for Everyone, 114
Needles, 17
   threading, 41-43
New Methods in Needlepoint, 114

Painting canvas, 36
Patch pockets. *See* Pockets
Pens, felt, 22
Persian wool, 10
Picken, Mary Brooks, 114
Pillows and cushions, 75-76
   designs, 25-28, 35, 39
   leftover canvas for, 16
   mounting, 101-6
   origin of ideas for shell, mini Op, 83
Pincushions
   as gifts, 87
   leftover canvas for, 16
Pins
   for blocking, 98
   for designing, 22
Pockets
   finishes, 113
   as gifts, 87
   leftover canvas for, 16
Proofreading needlepoint, 93
Purses, as gifts, 86
Pushpins. *See* Pins

Quick-point wool, 11

Restoring needlepoint, 113
Rugs, 76-77
   designing, 30-33
   mounting, 107
Rug wool, 11

Sandals, idea for strawberry, 83
Scissors, 17
Scotch stitch, 59-60
Scrap baskets, 79
Screens, 78

Seats, 76. *See also* Pillows and cushions
   designing, 38
   mounting slip, 104-5
Sidney, Sylvia, 114
Signatures, 23
Silk thread, 12
Slip seats, 76
   mounting, 104-5
Smyrna stitch, 58
Snook, Barbara, 114
Soap, liquid, 99
Stitches, 41-61
   basket-weave, 43-48
   brick, 50-53
   continental, 48-50
   flame, 55-57
   Florentine, 53
   Gobelin, 53-55
   herringbone, 57
   Scotch, 59-60
   Smyrna, 58
   triangle, 60-61
Sylvia Sidney Needlepoint Book, 114

Tables and table tops, 77-78
   mounting, 110-12
   utilizing canvas for, 6
Tassels, 66-67
Tapestry. *See* Wall hangings
Tapestry wool, 10-11
Thimbles, 17
Threading needles, 41-43
Tight seats, 76
Tonal values, 71
Tools and equipment, 17
   blocking, 98-99
   design, 22-23
Towels, for blocking, 99
Traveling, 84
Triangles, for blocking, 98
Triangle stitch, 60-61
Tweezers, 17

Wall hangings (tapestries), 78
   design for, 33-35
   mounting, 122
Washing needlepoint, 95
Water colors, 22
White (color), 70
White, Doris, 114
Williams, Elsa S., 57, 114
Wool, 8-15
   colors, 70-71
   hints on, 14-15
   how to buy, 12-13
   sorting and storing, 13-14
   substitutes for, 11-12
   types and uses, 10-11

Yellow, 70